EASY *to* ELEGANT

THE WORLD OF DOLE

Welcome to **Easy to Elegant**—the best of Dole. In the following pages you'll discover an array of exciting recipes inspired by exotic flavor combinations from around the world. These recipes reflect the carefree style of the Caribbean and the lure of the Hawaiian Islands; the warmth of New England hearthside dinners and the fun of Midwest backyard barbecues; the subtle mysteries of Asian cuisine; the luscious temptations of our devilishly good desserts . . . and much more. They've all been gathered here in one great collection featuring Dole's expanded line of wholesome, convenient products.

Easy to Elegant offers you a complete range of Dole recipes, from great breakfast and brunch ideas, superb salads and marvelous main dishes to thirst-quenching drinks and delightful desserts. There are easy-to-prepare dishes for everyday family meals and delicious creations special enough for company. Our "Entertaining with Style" section features complete menu suggestions to help you plan your next get-together. Entertaining is a natural for Dole. Pineapple, the traditional symbol of gracious hospitality, has been identified with the Dole name ever since Jim Dole planted his first pineapple in Hawaii. The flavorful fruit is depicted on doorways and bedposts; it even appears in European paintings of banquets dating back to the 1600s. Through the centuries, the pineapple has been recognized as an international sign for "Welcome to Our Home."

Today, the Dole family of products has grown to include bushels of fruit, from grapefruits, oranges and lemons to grapes, strawberries and bananas; refreshing breakfast juices; California-

grown almonds, pistachios, dates and raisins; a full selection of vegetables—lettuce, broccoli, cauliflower, carrots and celery to name only a few; fruit-fresh sorbets and frozen fruit bars for every taste. And, of course, our irreplaceable canned pineapple in syrup or its own tangy/ sweet juice.

We hope you enjoy these special recipes created with healthful, light ingredients from the world of Dole. A variety of internationally inspired flavors in special combinations and the enduring favorites of American home cooking are all at your fingertips.

BEST OF BRUNCH

EGGS D'ÉPINARDS

A delectable version of Eggs Benedict.

2 bunches (¾ pound each) fresh
   spinach, washed, trimmed
   and drained
2 tablespoons butter or margarine
2 tablespoons flour
½ teaspoon dried tarragon,
   crumbled
1⅓ cups milk
1 cup shredded sharp Cheddar
   cheese
   Salt
8 slices Canadian bacon or ham
8 eggs
2 cans (8 ounces each) Dole
   pineapple slices, drained

In large saucepan, cook spinach in
½ inch boiling water 3 minutes or until
bright green and wilted. Drain well;
keep warm. In small saucepan, melt
butter over medium heat; stir in
flour and tarragon. Cook, stirring
constantly, until foamy. Gradually stir
in milk; cook, stirring, until sauce is
smooth and thickened. Add cheese;
stir until melted. Add salt to taste.
   In lightly greased skillet, warm
Canadian bacon. In large skillet or
saucepan, poach eggs in 1½ inches
simmering water 3 to 4 minutes;
remove with slotted spoon. Arrange
spinach on 4 plates. For each serving,
top spinach with 2 slices Canadian
bacon, 2 pineapple slices and 2
poached eggs. Spoon cheese sauce
over all. Serve immediately.

Makes 4 servings

*Top right: Poppy Seed Bread (see page 6);
bottom: Eggs d'Épinards*

PINEAPPLE CITRUS MUFFINS

⅓ cup honey
¼ cup butter or margarine, softened
1 egg
1 can (8 ounces) Dole crushed pineapple
1 tablespoon grated orange peel
1 cup all-purpose flour
1 cup whole wheat flour
1½ teaspoons baking powder
¼ teaspoon salt
¼ teaspoon ground nutmeg
1 cup Dole chopped dates
½ cup chopped walnuts, optional

Preheat oven to 375°F. In large mixer bowl, beat together honey and butter 1 minute. Beat in egg, then undrained pineapple and orange peel. In medium bowl, combine remaining ingredients; stir into pineapple mixture until just blended. Spoon batter into 12 greased muffin cups. Bake in preheated oven 25 minutes or until wooden pick inserted in center comes out clean. Cool slightly in pan before turning out onto wire rack. Serve warm.

Makes 12 muffins

Pineapple Citrus Muffins

POPPY SEED BREAD

A delicious version of the classic banana bread.

1 cup sugar
½ cup butter or margarine, softened
2 eggs
1 teaspoon grated lemon peel
2 extra-ripe, medium Dole bananas
2 cups flour
2 teaspoons baking powder
½ teaspoon salt
¼ teaspoon ground cinnamon
¼ cup poppy seeds

Preheat oven to 350°F. In large bowl, beat sugar and butter until light and fluffy. Beat in eggs and lemon peel. Puree bananas in blender (1 cup). In small bowl, combine flour, baking powder, salt and cinnamon. Add dry ingredients to egg mixture alternately with pureed bananas, ending with dry ingredients. Stir in poppy seeds. Spoon into greased 9×5-inch loaf pan.

Bake in preheated oven 60 to 70 minutes or until wooden pick inserted in center comes out clean. Cool slightly in loaf pan before turning out onto wire rack to cool completely.

Makes 1 loaf

For a quick, nutritious breakfast or after-school snack, spread peanut butter on a toasted English muffin and top with banana slices.

Pineapple-Turkey Croissant Sandwich

PINEAPPLE-TURKEY CROISSANT SANDWICH

An elegant way to serve leftover turkey.

1 can (8 ounces) Dole pineapple
  slices
2 croissants
  Crisp Dole lettuce leaves
2 slices Swiss cheese
6 ounces sliced cooked turkey
½ cup cranberry sauce
¼ cup mayonnaise
¼ cup dairy sour cream
1 teaspoon grated orange peel

Drain pineapple. Slice croissants in half. On bottom half of each croissant, layer lettuce, cheese, turkey and pineapple. In small bowl, combine cranberry sauce, mayonnaise, sour cream and orange peel. Spoon sauce over sandwich filling. Top with croissant tops.

Makes 2 sandwiches

KENTUCKY SCRAMBLE

8 slices bacon
2 cups sliced fresh mushrooms
1 cup frozen whole-kernel corn,
    thawed
½ cup diced Dole green bell
    pepper
¼ cup diced pimento
    Salt
6 eggs
¼ cup water
2 tablespoons butter or margarine

In large skillet, fry bacon until crisp
and brown; drain on paper towels.
Pour off all but 2 tablespoons pan
drippings. Saute mushrooms and corn
in drippings. Add green pepper,
pimento and salt to taste; saute until
green pepper is soft.

Meanwhile, in medium bowl, beat
eggs with water. Melt butter in skillet
with vegetables. Pour in eggs and
scramble to desired doneness. Serve
with bacon.

Makes 4 servings

NUTTY BANANA
JAM MUFFINS

*These muffins have a sweet surprise in
the center.*

1¼ cups ground walnuts
1½ cups sugar
¾ cup butter or margarine,
    softened
2 extra-ripe, medium Dole
    bananas
1 egg
2 cups flour
2 teaspoons baking powder
1½ teaspoons ground cinnamon
½ teaspoon ground nutmeg
¼ teaspoon salt
1 ripe, small Dole banana
3 tablespoons raspberry jam

Preheat oven to 400°F. Line 18 muffin
cups with paper liners. In shallow dish,
combine ¾ cup walnuts with ½ cup
sugar; set aside.

In large bowl, beat remaining ½ cup
nuts with remaining 1 cup sugar and
butter until light and fluffy. Puree
2 medium bananas in blender (1 cup).
Beat pureed bananas and egg into
sugar-butter mixture. In medium
bowl, combine flour, baking powder,
cinnamon, nutmeg and salt. Beat dry
ingredients into banana mixture until
well mixed.

Mash small banana in small bowl;
stir in raspberry jam. For each muffin,
roll 1 heaping tablespoon dough in
walnut-sugar mixture to coat. Place in
lined muffin cup. Make a dimple in
center of dough with back of spoon.
Spoon 1 teaspoon jam mixture into
center. Roll 1 more heaping
tablespoon dough in walnut-sugar
mixture. Drop over jam mixture.
Repeat with remaining dough and jam
mixture.

Bake in preheated oven 15 to 20
minutes or until wooden pick inserted
in center comes out clean. Cool
slightly in pan before turning out onto
wire rack. Serve warm.

Makes 18 muffins

*Tired of peanut butter? Try almond but-
ter. Combine 2 cups toasted almonds
and 3 tablespoons vegetable oil in your
food processor. Process 2 to 3 minutes
or until smooth. Store, covered, in refrigerator.*

*Clockwise from top left: Nutty Banana Jam
Muffins; Ambrosia (see page 28);
Kentucky Scramble*

Left: Fruit Festival; right: Mandarin Orange French Toast

MANDARIN ORANGE FRENCH TOAST

Serve with ham or Canadian bacon.

**1 can (11 ounces) Dole Mandarin
   orange segments**
1 tablespoon grated orange peel
½ cup orange juice
1 tablespoon brown sugar
2 teaspoons cornstarch
**1 teaspoon vanilla extract
   Dash ground nutmeg**
2 eggs, lightly beaten
½ cup half-and-half
**4 slices (½ inch thick each) stale
   French bread or thick-sliced
   white bread**
2 tablespoons butter or margarine
**¼ cup Dole sliced natural
   almonds, toasted, optional**

Drain syrup from oranges into saucepan. Stir in orange peel and juice, brown sugar, cornstarch, vanilla and nutmeg. Cook over low heat, stirring, until sauce thickens slightly and turns clear. Remove from heat; add orange segments.

In pie plate, combine eggs and half-and-half. Dip bread in egg mixture, saturating both sides. Melt butter in large skillet until hot. Cook soaked bread in skillet until golden brown on each side. Place 2 slices French toast on each plate; top with Mandarin orange sauce. Sprinkle with almonds, if desired.

Makes 2 servings

FRUIT FESTIVAL

1 Dole fresh pineapple
1 firm, medium Dole banana
1 apple, cored and cubed
1 small Dole orange, peeled and
   sliced
½ cup cubed melon
   Brown sugar
½ teaspoon grated lime peel
   Juice of 1 lime

Twist crown from pineapple. Cut
pineapple lengthwise into quarters.
Remove fruit from shells with curved
knife. Trim off core and cut fruit into
chunks. Slice banana. In medium
bowl, combine 2 cups pineapple with
banana, apple, orange and melon.
(Refrigerate remaining pineapple for
another use.) Sprinkle fruit with brown
sugar, lime peel and juice.
Makes 2 servings

OMELET AUX FRUITS

3 eggs
1 teaspoon grated orange peel
1 tablespoon fresh orange juice
¼ teaspoon salt
1 tablespoon butter or margarine
1 ripe, medium Dole banana
1 tablespoon Dole raisins
¼ cup plain yogurt, optional
1 tablespoon chutney, optional

In large bowl, beat together eggs,
orange peel, orange juice and salt.
Melt butter in 6-inch omelet pan over
medium-high heat. Pour egg mixture
into omelet pan; cook, lifting omelet
edge to let uncooked egg flow
underneath. While top is still moist,
slice banana onto omelet and sprinkle
with raisins. Fold omelet in half and
serve on warmed plate. Top with
yogurt and chutney, if desired.
Makes 2 servings

BANANA NUT PANCAKES

A family Sunday breakfast favorite.

2 ripe, medium Dole bananas
¾ cup milk
1 egg, lightly beaten
1 tablespoon vegetable oil
1 cup pancake and waffle mix
½ cup chopped walnuts
⅛ teaspoon ground cinnamon
   Banana slices and additional
   chopped nuts

Mash bananas in medium bowl
(1 cup). Stir in milk, egg and oil. In
medium bowl, combine pancake mix,
nuts and cinnamon. Stir banana
mixture into dry ingredients until just
moistened. For each pancake, pour
¼ cup batter onto lightly greased hot
skillet. Brown on underside until
bubbles appear on surface. Turn and
brown other side. Serve with banana
slices and additional nuts.
Makes 4 to 5 servings

Banana Nut Pancakes

PINEAPPLE BRUNCH CASSEROLE

A perfect use for leftover ham.

1 can (8 ounces) Dole crushed
    pineapple
1 cup biscuit mix
1 cup milk
4 eggs, lightly beaten
6 tablespoons butter or
    margarine, melted
1 teaspoon Dijon mustard
½ teaspoon onion powder
    Pinch ground nutmeg
4 ounces cooked ham, diced
1 cup shredded Monterey Jack or
    sharp Cheddar cheese
2 green onions, finely chopped

Preheat oven to 350°F. Drain
pineapple. Reserve 2 tablespoons
pineapple for garnish, if desired.
Combine biscuit mix, milk, eggs,
butter, mustard, onion powder and
nutmeg in blender or in large mixer
bowl until smooth. Stir in ham,
cheese, onions and pineapple. Pour
into greased 9-inch pie plate. Bake in
preheated oven 35 to 40 minutes or
until set. Garnish with reserved
pineapple, if desired.

Makes 6 servings

PINEAPPLE NUT BUTTER

1 can (8¼ ounces) Dole crushed
    pineapple
⅓ cup peanut butter

Drain pineapple. In small bowl,
combine pineapple and peanut butter.
Use to serve on toast or English
muffins. Store in covered container in
refrigerator.

Makes 1 cup

Pineapple Brunch Casserole

Gingery Banana Waffles

GINGERY BANANA WAFFLES

A spicy, old-fashioned waffle for fall and winter breakfasts.

      3 cups flour
      4 teaspoons baking powder
      2 teaspoons ground cinnamon
  1½ teaspoons ground ginger
      1 teaspoon salt
      4 eggs
  ⅔ cup brown sugar, packed
      2 extra-ripe, medium Dole
           bananas
  1¼ cups milk
  ½ cup molasses
  ½ cup butter or margarine, melted
      4 firm, medium Dole bananas,
           sliced
         Maple syrup

Preheat waffle iron. In large bowl, combine flour, baking powder, cinnamon, ginger and salt. In medium bowl, beat eggs with brown sugar until light and fluffy. Puree extra-ripe bananas in blender (1 cup). Beat pureed bananas, milk, molasses and butter into egg mixture; add to dry ingredients. Stir until just moistened.

For each waffle, cook ¾ cup batter in waffle iron until golden brown. Serve with sliced bananas and syrup.

Makes 8 servings

SESAME CRUNCH BANANA MUFFINS

A satisfying muffin with a spicy nut topping.

2 ripe, medium Dole bananas
1 cup milk
1 egg
¼ cup vegetable oil
1 teaspoon vanilla extract
1½ cups quick-cooking rolled oats
½ cup all-purpose flour
½ cup whole wheat flour
1 tablespoon baking powder
½ teaspoon salt
Sesame Crunch (recipe follows)

Preheat oven to 400°F. Puree bananas in blender (1 cup). In large bowl, combine pureed bananas, milk, egg, oil and vanilla; set aside. In large bowl, combine oats, flours, baking powder and salt. Stir in banana mixture just until dry ingredients are moistened (batter will be lumpy). Fill 12 greased muffin cups about ¾ full. Sprinkle 2 teaspoons Sesame Crunch over batter in each cup. Bake in preheated oven 20 to 25 minutes or until golden on top and wooden pick inserted in center comes out clean. Cool slightly in pan before turning out onto wire rack. Serve warm.

Makes 12 muffins

Sesame Crunch: In small bowl, combine ¼ cup chopped nuts, 2 tablespoons *each* brown sugar and sesame seeds, 1 tablespoon whole wheat flour and ¼ teaspoon *each* ground cinnamon and nutmeg. Cut in 2 tablespoons butter or margarine until crumbly.

Sesame Crunch Banana Muffins

JAMAICAN TOAST

2 ripe, medium Dole bananas
1 egg
1 teaspoon ground cinnamon
Dash salt
6 slices (1 inch thick each) stale Italian or French bread
1 tablespoon butter or margarine
½ cup flaked coconut, toasted
½ cup Dole sliced natural almonds

Mash bananas in large bowl until smooth. Beat in egg, cinnamon and salt. Dip bread into banana mixture, saturating both sides. Melt butter in large skillet over medium-high heat. Cook bread in skillet until golden brown on each side. Sprinkle with toasted coconut and almonds.

Makes 2 to 3 servings

BANANA COFFEE CAKE

6 tablespoons butter or
    margarine, softened
¾ cup sugar
1 egg
1 tablespoon grated lemon peel
1 teaspoon vanilla extract
½ cup milk
2 cups flour
1 tablespoon baking powder
¼ teaspoon salt
3 large, ripe Dole bananas
    Streusel Topping (recipe follows)

Preheat oven to 375°F. In large bowl, beat butter and sugar until light and fluffy. Beat in egg, lemon peel and vanilla until smooth. Stir in milk. In small bowl, combine flour, baking powder and salt; add to butter mixture, stirring until blended. Slice bananas (3 cups); fold into batter. Spoon batter into greased 9-inch square baking pan. Smooth top. Sprinkle with Streusel Topping. Bake in preheated oven 45 to 50 minutes or until wooden pick inserted in center comes out clean. Cool on wire rack 20 minutes before cutting.
Makes 9 servings

Streusel Topping: In medium bowl, combine ⅓ cup packed brown sugar, ⅓ cup flour and ¾ teaspoon ground cinnamon. Cut in ¼ cup butter or margarine until mixture is crumbly.

Banana Breakfast Spread

Brighten your next breakfast or brunch with Dole pineapple slices. Their sweet-tart flavor complements smoked meats such as ham or bacon. Either saute to heat or serve at room temperature.

BANANA BREAKFAST SPREAD

Kids love it—it's quick and easy, too.

2 ripe, medium Dole bananas
1 cup chunky peanut butter
¼ cup mayonnaise
¼ cup Dole raisins
¼ teaspoon ground cinnamon
    Toasted bread or English
    muffins
    Honey or jam, optional

Slice bananas into bowl. Stir in peanut butter, mayonnaise, raisins and cinnamon. Spread desired amount on toast. Drizzle with honey or jam, if desired. Store spread in covered container in refrigerator.
Makes 2 cups

SUPER
SALADS

FRUIT SALAD WITH ORANGE ALMOND DRESSING

Toasted almonds accent a colorful melange of fresh fruit.

1 head Dole leaf lettuce
1 Dole orange, peeled and
   sectioned
1 peach, sliced
½ cantaloupe, cut into chunks
2 cups Dole fresh pineapple
   chunks
1 cup sliced Dole strawberries
1 cup Dole grapes
½ cup Dole whole natural
   almonds, toasted
   Orange Almond Dressing
   (recipe follows)

Line large salad bowl with lettuce
leaves. Arrange fruit on top; sprinkle
with almonds. Serve with Orange
Almond Dressing.

Makes 6 to 8 servings

Orange Almond Dressing: In
1-quart measure, combine 1 cup dairy
sour cream, ½ cup mayonnaise,
¼ cup toasted Dole chopped natural
almonds, 2 tablespoons lemon juice
and 2 teaspoons grated orange peel.
Refrigerate, covered, until ready to
serve.

*Left: Fruit Salad with Orange Almond
Dressing; right: Dole's Summer Vegetable
Salad (see page 18)*

DOLE'S SUMMER VEGETABLE SALAD

1 head Dole lettuce
2 Dole tomatoes
1 cucumber
½ Dole red bell pepper
¼ red onion
1 cup sliced Dole celery
1 cup snow peas, ends and strings removed
1 cup sliced Dole cauliflower
  Dill Dressing (recipe follows)

Tear lettuce into bite-size pieces. Cut tomatoes into wedges. Slice cucumber, red pepper and red onion. Toss all vegetables in salad bowl with Dill Dressing.

Makes 4 servings

Dill Dressing: In 1-quart measure, combine ½ cup *each* dairy sour cream and mayonnaise, 1 tablespoon vinegar, 1 teaspoon *each* dried dill weed and onion powder, 1 teaspoon Dijon mustard, ¾ teaspoon garlic salt and cracked pepper to taste. Refrigerate, covered, until ready to serve.

CITRUS SALAD PLATTER

Fruit and cheese make ideal partners for appetizers, snacks or desserts.

2 firm, medium Dole bananas, sliced
2 Dole oranges, peeled and sectioned
1 Dole grapefruit, peeled and sectioned
1 avocado, sliced
  Fresh Dole spinach leaves
4 ounces Brie, Swiss or Cheddar cheese
  Poppy Seed Dressing (recipe follows)
  French bread, optional

Arrange fruit and avocado on spinach-lined platter. Place cheese in center of platter or on separate cheese board. Serve with Poppy Seed Dressing, and French bread, if desired.

Makes 4 servings

Poppy Seed Dressing: Combine ¾ cup sugar, ⅓ cup white vinegar, 1½ tablespoons finely chopped onion and 1 teaspoon *each* salt and dry mustard in blender until sugar dissolves. Slowly pour in 1 cup vegetable oil while blending on medium speed. Blend until thickened. Stir in 1½ tablespoons poppy seeds. Refrigerate, covered, until ready to serve.

CURRIED PINEAPPLE PASTA SALAD

Serve this hearty pasta salad without the chicken as a side dish.

1 can (20 ounces) Dole pineapple chunks
2 cups cooked, shredded chicken
8 ounces macaroni or other small pasta, cooked
2 cups sliced Dole celery
½ cup sliced green onion
½ cup julienne-cut Dole red bell pepper
½ cup sliced ripe olives
¾ cup mayonnaise
⅓ cup chopped chutney
¼ cup dairy sour cream
2 teaspoons curry powder
1 teaspoon salt

Drain pineapple. In salad bowl, combine pineapple, chicken, pasta, celery, onion, red pepper and olives. To make dressing, in 1-quart measure, combine remaining ingredients; toss with salad. Refrigerate, covered, until ready to serve.

Makes 8 servings

Pineapple Turkey Salad

PINEAPPLE TURKEY SALAD

A creative use for leftover turkey.

1 can (8 ounces) Dole pineapple
   chunks or tidbits
2 cups cubed cooked turkey
1 cup sliced Dole celery
¼ cup low-calorie mayonnaise
   Crisp Dole lettuce leaves
¼ cup whole berry cranberry sauce
2 tablespoons Dole blanched
   slivered almonds, toasted
½ pound Dole seedless grapes
1 Dole orange, sliced

Drain pineapple. In large bowl,
combine pineapple, turkey, celery and
mayonnaise. Line salad plates with
lettuce leaves. Place turkey salad in
center of each plate. Top with
cranberry sauce and toasted almonds.
Arrange grapes and orange slices
around turkey salad.

Makes 3 to 4 servings

MAUI FRUIT SALAD

A colorful blend of fruit with a lime-yogurt dressing.

1 Dole fresh pineapple
1 papaya, peeled, seeded and
   sliced
1 large Dole banana, sliced
1 cup halved Dole strawberries
1 carton (8 ounces) vanilla yogurt
½ teaspoon grated lime peel
1 tablespoon fresh lime juice
1 teaspoon honey

Twist crown from pineapple. Cut
pineapple lengthwise into quarters.
Remove fruit from shells with curved
knife. Trim off core and cut fruit into
chunks. In large bowl, combine
pineapple, papaya, banana and
strawberries. To make dressing, in
1-quart measure, combine remaining
ingredients. Serve fruit salad with
dressing.

Makes 6 to 8 servings

Holiday Fruit Salad

HOLIDAY FRUIT SALAD

A colorful addition to a holiday buffet dinner.

3 packages (3 ounces each) strawberry flavor gelatin
3 cups boiling water
2 ripe Dole bananas
1 package (16 ounces) frozen strawberries
1 can (20 ounces) Dole crushed pineapple
1 package (8 ounces) cream cheese, softened
1 cup dairy sour cream or plain yogurt
¼ cup sugar
Crisp Dole lettuce leaves

In large bowl, dissolve gelatin in boiling water. Slice bananas into gelatin mixture. Add frozen strawberries and undrained pineapple. Pour half the mixture into 13×9-inch pan. Refrigerate 1 hour or until firm. In mixer bowl, beat cream cheese with sour cream and sugar; spread over chilled layer. Gently spoon remaining gelatin mixture on top. Refrigerate until firm, about 2 hours. Cut into squares; serve on lettuce-lined salad plates. Garnish with additional pineapple, if desired.

Makes 12 servings

LYNN'S SALAD

1 head Dole cauliflower, cut into flowerets
1 bunch Dole broccoli, cut into flowerets
1 jar (6 ounces) marinated artichoke hearts, drained
8 ounces mozzarella cheese, cubed
2 cups pitted ripe olives
Dash garlic salt
1 bottle (8 ounces) Italian salad dressing

In large bowl, combine cauliflower, broccoli, artichokes, cheese, olives and garlic salt. Pour salad dressing over vegetable mixture. Refrigerate, covered, overnight. Drain salad dressing (save for another use, if desired).

Makes 6 servings

COUNTRY PINEAPPLE SLAW

1 can (20 ounces) Dole pineapple chunks
1 package (16 ounces) Dole cole slaw mix
½ cup sunflower seeds
Zesty Dressing (recipe follows)

Drain pineapple. In large bowl, combine pineapple with cole slaw mix and sunflower seeds. Toss with Zesty Dressing. Refrigerate, covered, until ready to serve.

Makes 6 servings

Zesty Dressing: In 1-quart measure, combine ½ cup *each* mayonnaise and dairy sour cream, 2 tablespoons lemon juice, 1 tablespoon Dijon mustard and ½ teaspoon caraway seeds. Blend well.

Ripe pineapple comes in a variety of colors from green to gold. It is picked from the field when ripe and does not ripen further as do other fruits.

INDIAN FRUIT SALAD

1 Dole fresh pineapple
2 firm Dole bananas
1 head Dole iceberg lettuce, torn
1 Dole orange, peeled and sliced
2 cups melon balls or diced melon
½ cup cashew nuts
1 cup mayonnaise
¼ cup dairy sour cream
1 tablespoon fresh lime juice
1 tablespoon sugar
1 teaspoon curry powder
½ teaspoon grated lime peel
½ teaspoon salt

Twist crown from pineapple. Cut pineapple lengthwise into quarters. Remove fruit from shells with curved knife. Trim off core and dice fruit. Slice bananas into large bowl. Add 2½ cups pineapple (reserve remaining pineapple for another use), lettuce, orange, melon and nuts. To make dressing, in 1-quart measure, combine remaining ingredients; refrigerate, covered, until ready to serve. Pour dressing over salad and toss.

Makes 6 to 8 servings

Indian Fruit Salad

Calypso Shrimp Salad

CALYPSO SHRIMP SALAD

An exotic dressing of banana and chutney gives this salad a Caribbean flair.

1 cantaloupe, peeled and sliced into 4 rings
Crisp Dole lettuce leaves
1 pound frozen salad shrimp, thawed
2 firm Dole bananas, sliced
1 Dole orange, peeled and sliced
1 pound Dole red grapes, cut into clusters
Banana Chutney Dressing (recipe follows)

Arrange each cantaloupe ring on lettuce-lined salad plate. Fill centers with shrimp. Arrange banana slices, orange slices and grapes around cantaloupe. Serve with Banana Chutney Dressing.

Makes 4 servings

Banana Chutney Dressing: Puree 1 ripe Dole banana in blender. Add ½ cup mayonnaise, 2 tablespoons chutney and 1 tablespoon lemon juice. Process until blended. Refrigerate, covered, until ready to serve.

Fresh pineapple is picked at the peak of ripeness, so you should use it as soon as possible after purchase. Don't keep it out on the kitchen counter for longer than a few days, and please keep it out of the sun!

CALIFORNIA SALAD

A date-curry dressing gives this salad its unique flavor.

1 Dole fresh pineapple
1 head Dole iceberg lettuce
2 Dole bananas, sliced
8 ounces Dole grapes
2 Dole carrots, sliced
1 Dole tomato, cut into wedges
½ cucumber, sliced
2 stalks Dole celery, sliced
¼ cup Dole whole natural
   almonds, toasted
Date Dressing (recipe follows)

Twist crown from pineapple. Cut pineapple lengthwise into quarters. Remove fruit with curved knife. Trim off core and cut fruit into thin wedges. Line serving platter with lettuce leaves. Arrange half the pineapple and remaining fruits and vegetables on lettuce (reserve remaining pineapple for another use). Sprinkle with almonds. Serve with Date Dressing.
Makes 6 servings

Date Dressing: In 1-quart measure, combine ⅔ cup vegetable oil, ¼ cup raspberry vinegar, 1 tablespoon sugar, 2 teaspoons soy sauce, 1 teaspoon *each* curry powder and dry mustard and ½ teaspoon garlic salt. Stir in ⅓ cup Dole chopped dates.

PIÑATA SALAD

Let your guests choose their salad toppings and dressing.

1 head Dole iceberg lettuce, torn
1 avocado, diced
1 can (16 ounces) garbanzo
   beans, drained
1 cup diced Dole tomatoes
1 cup ripe olives, cut into wedges
   or sliced
1 cup sliced Dole celery
1 cup sliced jicama or radishes
4 ounces sharp Cheddar cheese,
   shredded
Gazpacho Dressing (recipe
   follows)
Chile Dressing (recipe follows)

Place lettuce in salad bowl. Place avocado, garbanzo beans, tomatoes, olives, celery, jicama and cheese in individual bowls for a choice of toppings. Serve with either Gazpacho or Chile Dressing.
Makes 6 to 8 servings

Gazpacho Dressing: In screw-top jar, combine ½ cup olive or vegetable oil, ¼ cup vinegar, 3 sliced green onions, ¾ cup diced tomato, ¼ cup diced green bell pepper, 1 pressed garlic clove, 3 tablespoons chopped cilantro or parsley, 1 teaspoon salt and 6 drops liquid hot pepper seasoning. Shake well to combine.

Chile Dressing: Puree 7 ounces (1 can) diced green chiles, 1 cup mayonnaise and ¼ cup dairy sour cream in blender. Refrigerate, covered, until ready to serve.

Piñata Salad

Pineapple Spinach Salad

Canned drained pineapple, either crushed or tidbits, is a tasty addition to basic chicken salad.

STAY SLIM SALAD

2 cups shredded Dole iceberg
  lettuce
¼ cup chopped green onion
½ pound sliced cooked chicken
2 small Dole bananas, sliced
1 large Dole pink grapefruit,
  peeled and sectioned
1 cup halved cherry tomatoes
½ cup sliced Dole celery
  Low-Calorie Dressing (recipe
  follows)

In medium bowl, combine lettuce and onion. Arrange on 2 salad plates. Arrange chicken in center of each. Arrange bananas, grapefruit, tomatoes and celery around chicken. Serve with Low-Calorie Dressing.

Makes 2 servings

Low-Calorie Dressing: In screw-top jar, combine ¼ cup lime juice, 2 tablespoons vegetable oil, 2 teaspoons sugar, ½ teaspoon paprika and ¼ teaspoon *each* salt and dry mustard. Shake until well blended.

Stay Slim Salad

PINEAPPLE SPINACH SALAD

1 Dole fresh pineapple
1 bunch Dole fresh spinach leaves
4 bacon strips, cooked and
  crumbled
2 hard-cooked eggs, chopped
1 red onion, sliced
  Basil Dressing (recipe follows)

Twist crown from pineapple. Cut pineapple lengthwise into quarters. Remove fruit from shell with curved knife. Trim off core and cut fruit into chunks. In large bowl, combine pineapple, spinach, bacon, eggs and onion. Toss with Basil Dressing. Serve immediately on chilled salad plates.

Makes 4 servings

Basil Dressing: In 1-quart measure, combine 6 tablespoons vegetable oil, 2 tablespoons white wine vinegar, 1 teaspoon crumbled dried basil and ½ teaspoon dry mustard. Blend well.

Mai Tai Compote

MAI TAI COMPOTE

Pineapple boats make beautiful containers for this colorful salad.

1 medium Dole fresh pineapple
1 Dole orange, peeled and sliced
1 kiwifruit, peeled and sliced
1 cup halved Dole strawberries
½ cup seedless Dole red grapes
¼ cup fresh lime juice
3 tablespoons honey
1 tablespoon light rum
1 tablespoon orange-flavored liqueur
½ teaspoon grated lime peel
1 firm Dole banana

Cut pineapple in half lengthwise through crown. Remove fruit with curved knife, leaving shells intact. Trim off core and cut fruit into chunks. In large bowl, combine pineapple, orange, kiwi, strawberries and grapes. To make dressing, in 1-quart measure, combine remaining ingredients, except banana. Pour dressing over fruit. Toss gently to coat. Refrigerate, covered, 1 hour. Just before serving, slice banana into fruit salad. Toss gently. Spoon salad into pineapple shells and serve.

Makes 6 to 8 servings

DOLE'S CHEF SALAD

A delectable combination with a savory dressing.

1 can (20 ounces) Dole pineapple tidbits
Crisp Dole salad greens
8 ounces cooked ham, julienne-cut
8 ounces Cheddar cheese, cut into chunks
4 ounces bean sprouts, optional
1 jar (6 ounces) marinated artichoke hearts, drained
1 Dole red bell pepper, seeded and sliced
Ripe olives
Pesto Dressing (recipe follows)

Drain pineapple. Arrange salad greens in large bowl or platter. Arrange pineapple, ham, cheese, bean sprouts, artichoke hearts, red pepper and olives on top. Serve with Pesto Dressing.

Makes 4 servings

Pesto Dressing: Puree 1½ cups fresh basil leaves, ½ cup mayonnaise, 3 tablespoons olive oil, 3 tablespoons grated Parmesan cheese and 1 clove garlic in blender or food processor.

Tarragon Chicken Salad

TARRAGON CHICKEN SALAD

4 small avocados
  Crisp Dole salad greens
2 firm, small Dole bananas
2 cups cooked diced chicken
1 Dole orange, peeled and cut into
  bite-size pieces
1 Dole red bell pepper, seeded and
  diced
  Creamy Tarragon Dressing
  (recipe follows)

Peel avocados and cut into halves; remove seeds. Place avocado halves on 4 salad plates lined with salad greens. Slice bananas into bowl; add chicken, orange and red pepper. Toss together. Fill each avocado half with chicken salad. Garnish with additional fruit slices, if desired. Serve with Creamy Tarragon Dressing.

Makes 4 servings

Creamy Tarragon Dressing: In 1-quart measure, combine ¾ cup mayonnaise, 2 teaspoons Dijon mustard, 1 teaspoon red wine vinegar, 1 teaspoon dried tarragon and salt and pepper to taste. Refrigerate, covered, until ready to serve.

GINGER FRUIT SALAD

1 Dole fresh pineapple
1 firm Dole banana
1 apple, cored and cut into
  chunks
1 Dole orange, peeled and cut into
  bite-size pieces
1 cup seedless Dole grapes
¼ cup vegetable oil
1 ripe, small Dole banana
1 tablespoon chopped crystallized
  ginger
1 teaspoon grated orange peel

Cut pineapple into halves lengthwise through crown. Remove fruit from shell with curved knife, leaving shell intact. Trim off core and cut fruit into chunks. Reserve 1 cup pineapple for dressing. Slice firm banana into large bowl; add remaining pineapple, apple, orange and grapes. Spoon into pineapple shells. To make dressing, pour oil into blender. Gradually add 1 cup reserved pineapple while blending at medium speed. Add remaining ingredients; blend well. Serve dressing over fruit.

Makes 4 servings

ITALIAN-STYLE CAULIFLOWER SALAD

1 head Dole cauliflower, cut into
  flowerets
½ cup olive or vegetable oil
¼ cup vinegar
1 clove garlic, pressed
½ teaspoon salt
½ teaspoon cracked black pepper
¼ teaspoon dried basil, crumbled
1 cup sliced Dole green or red bell
  pepper
1 cup sliced Dole celery
1 cup sliced Dole carrots
½ cup sliced pimento-stuffed olives
¼ cup chopped parsley

In large saucepan, cook cauliflower in steamer basket over boiling water 8 minutes or until tender-crisp. Drain; transfer to large bowl. To make dressing, in 1-quart measure, combine oil, vinegar, garlic, salt, pepper and basil. Pour dressing over warm cauliflower. Add remaining ingredients; toss to coat. Refrigerate, covered, overnight.

Makes 6 servings

PINEAPPLE AND HAM PASTA SALAD

1 can (20 ounces) Dole pineapple
  tidbits
1 pound cooked ham, diced
1 Dole red or green bell pepper,
  seeded and diced
2 cups frozen peas, thawed
2 cups diced Dole celery
8 ounces elbow macaroni, cooked
1¼ cups mayonnaise
1 tablespoon vinegar
1 teaspoon onion powder
¼ teaspoon pepper
¼ teaspoon dried dill weed

Drain pineapple. In large bowl, combine pineapple, ham, red pepper, peas, celery and macaroni. To make dressing, in 1-quart measure, combine mayonnaise, vinegar, onion powder, pepper and dill weed. Stir dressing into pineapple mixture. Refrigerate 3 to 4 hours before serving to allow flavors to blend.

Makes 8 servings

To give extra flavor to soups, add leftover vegetables. Save vegetable leftovers, even lettuce, in a container in the freezer. When you're ready to make soup, simply add the leftovers to canned chicken broth or beef broth and simmer until soup is ready.

Pineapple and Ham Pasta Salad

HONG KONG SALAD

A touch of soy sauce and sesame seeds gives this salad its Oriental flavor.

1 bunch Dole broccoli, cut into flowerets (2 cups)
8 ounces snow peas, ends and strings removed
1 head Dole iceberg lettuce, torn
2 cups sliced Dole celery
½ Dole red bell pepper, seeded and sliced
1 bunch green onions, sliced
1 can (8 ounces) water chestnuts, sliced
Soy Dressing (recipe follows)

To blanch vegetables, cover broccoli and snow peas with boiling water. Let stand 5 minutes. Rinse under cold running water to stop cooking; drain. In salad bowl, combine broccoli and snow peas with remaining vegetables. Toss with Soy Dressing.

Makes 6 servings

Soy Dressing: In 1-quart measure, combine ½ cup vegetable oil, 3 tablespoons *each* soy sauce and vinegar, 1 pressed garlic clove, 1 tablespoon *each* sugar and toasted sesame seeds, ½ teaspoon ground ginger, ¼ teaspoon salt and pepper to taste. Blend well.

Ambrosia

LIGHT COBB SALAD FOR TWO

½ head Dole iceberg lettuce
½ chicken breast, cooked and shredded
2 slices bacon, cooked and crumbled
3 tablespoons crumbled blue cheese
1 Dole tomato, cut into wedges
1 cup chopped Dole broccoli
Bottled light French or Italian salad dressing

Tear lettuce into bite-size pieces; arrange on 2 salad plates. Arrange chicken down center in a straight line. Arrange bacon and blue cheese alongside of chicken. Garnish with tomato and broccoli. Serve with salad dressing.

Makes 2 servings

AMBROSIA

1 can (20 ounces) Dole pineapple chunks
1 can (11 ounces) Dole Mandarin orange segments
1 firm, large Dole banana, sliced, optional
1½ cups Dole seedless grapes
1 cup miniature marshmallows
1 cup flaked coconut
½ cup pecan halves or coarsely chopped nuts
1 cup dairy sour cream or plain yogurt
1 tablespoon brown sugar

Drain pineapple and orange segments. In large bowl, combine pineapple, mandarin oranges, banana, grapes, marshmallows, coconut and nuts. In 1-quart measure, combine sour cream and brown sugar. Stir into fruit mixture. Refrigerate, covered, 1 hour or overnight.

Makes 4 servings

Celery makes a versatile appetizer. Eat it plain, or dip it in a variety of sauces, or stuff the stalks with flavored cheese spreads.

Hospitality Salad

SEA SALAD

1 bunch Dole broccoli, cut into flowerets (2 cups)
4 ounces snow peas, ends and strings removed
8 ounces shell-shaped pasta
2 cups sliced Dole celery
2 cups sliced fresh mushrooms
½ cup sliced Dole red bell pepper
8 ounces cooked, shelled shrimp (see page 33)
Lemon-Mustard Dressing (recipe follows)

To blanch vegetables, cover broccoli and snow peas with boiling water. Let stand 5 minutes. Rinse under cold running water to stop cooking; drain. Cook pasta according to package directions; drain. In large bowl, combine vegetables, pasta and shrimp; toss with Lemon-Mustard Dressing. Refrigerate, covered, at least 2 hours before serving.

Makes 4 servings

Lemon-Mustard Dressing: In 1-quart measure, combine ½ cup olive or vegetable oil, 3 tablespoons lemon juice, 1 tablespoon wine vinegar, 2 teaspoons Dijon mustard, 1 teaspoon dried dill weed, ¼ teaspoon pepper and salt to taste. Blend well.

HOSPITALITY SALAD

1 can (20 ounces) Dole pineapple chunks
1 can (11 ounces) Dole Mandarin orange segments
8 ounces cooked ham, cut into strips
½ cup sliced water chestnuts
½ cup sliced cucumber
¼ cup sliced green onion
½ cup mayonnaise
½ teaspoon dried dill weed
1 avocado, diced
Crisp Dole salad greens

Drain pineapple; reserve 1 tablespoon liquid. Drain orange segments. In large bowl, combine pineapple, oranges, ham, water chestnuts, cucumber and green onion. To make dressing, in 1-quart measure, combine mayonnaise, dill weed and reserved liquid; toss with salad. Fold in avocado. Serve on salad plates lined with salad greens.

Makes 4 to 6 servings

Canned, sliced pineapple makes a terrific addition to grilled ham and cheese sandwiches.

INTERNATIONAL FAVORITES

PINEAPPLE CHICKEN MADEIRA

Elegant and easy to prepare.

1 can (8 ounces) Dole pineapple
   slices
1 whole chicken breast, split,
   skinned and boned
2 tablespoons flour
   Salt
2 tablespoons butter or margarine
½ cup julienne-cut Dole red bell
   pepper
2 green onions, sliced
3 tablespoons Madeira wine or
   sherry
½ cup whipping cream

Drain pineapple; reserve 2
tablespoons juice. Pound chicken to
½-inch thickness. Dredge chicken in
flour and salt to taste. In skillet, saute
chicken in butter on each side until
lightly browned, about 3 minutes. Add
reserved juice, red pepper, onions and
wine to skillet. Simmer 5 minutes.
Remove chicken to serving platter. Stir
cream into pan juices. Cook until
liquid is reduced, about 1 minute; add
pineapple and heat through. Top
chicken with pineapple and sauce.

Makes 2 servings

Pineapple Chicken Madeira

TERIYAKI FISH FILLETS

The essence of Oriental simplicity and subtle flavoring.

1 can (20 ounces) Dole pineapple
  chunks
1 clove garlic, pressed
2 tablespoons slivered fresh
  ginger root
1 tablespoon minced green onion
5 teaspoons teriyaki sauce
1 teaspoon white vinegar
1 pound sole fillets
2 teaspoons cornstarch
1 teaspoon minced fresh ginger
  root
1 teaspoon sesame oil

Measure 2 tablespoons juice from pineapple can; mix with garlic, slivered ginger, onion, 3 teaspoons teriyaki sauce and vinegar. Arrange fish in shallow dish. Pour marinade over fish. Refrigerate 10 minutes. Arrange fish on greased broiler rack. Brush with marinade. Broil 6 inches from heat 5 to 6 minutes. In saucepan, combine remaining 2 teaspoons teriyaki sauce, undrained pineapple and remaining ingredients. Cook until sauce boils and thickens. Serve with fish.

Makes 4 servings

POLYNESIAN VEGETABLES

A great microwave vegetable side dish. The leftovers may be served as a salad.

1 can (20 ounces) Dole pineapple
  chunks
½ cup chopped onion
2 cloves garlic, pressed
3 tablespoons soy sauce
1 tablespoon sesame oil
1 tablespoon cornstarch
½ teaspoon salt
2 Dole carrots, thinly sliced on
  diagonal (2 cups)
1 bunch Dole broccoli, cut into
  flowerets (2 cups)
1 Dole red or green bell pepper,
  seeded and cut into chunks
2 to 3 tablespoons sesame seeds,
  toasted

Drain pineapple juice into 2½-quart microwave-safe casserole dish. Stir in onion, garlic, soy sauce, oil, cornstarch and salt. Microwave on HIGH about 4 minutes, stirring after 2 minutes. Add carrots; stir to coat. Cover. Microwave on HIGH 5 to 6 minutes. Stir in broccoli and bell pepper; microwave on HIGH 3 to 5 minutes longer or until vegetables are tender-crisp. Remove cover. Stir in pineapple; continue microwaving on HIGH 2 to 3 minutes. Let stand 5 minutes before serving. Sprinkle with sesame seeds.

Makes 6 servings

Festival Shrimp

FESTIVAL SHRIMP

A unique shrimp dish featuring south-of-the-border flavors.

 1 Dole fresh pineapple
 1 large Dole tomato, cut into
   quarters
 1 medium onion, cut into quarters
 1 jar (4 ounces) pimentos
 ¼ cup canned diced green chiles
 2 tablespoons lime juice
 1½ teaspoons ground coriander
 1 teaspoon garlic salt
 1 teaspoon sugar
 ¼ cup butter or margarine
 1 pound medium shrimp, cooked
   and shelled*
 1 tablespoon chopped fresh
   cilantro or parsley
   Hot cooked rice

Twist crown from pineapple. Cut pineapple lengthwise into quarters. Remove fruit from shell with curved knife. Trim off core and cut fruit into chunks. Set aside.

In food processor or blender, combine tomato, onion, pimentos, green chiles, lime juice, coriander, garlic salt and sugar. Process until pureed.

In large skillet, melt butter. Add pureed sauce and simmer 5 minutes. Stir in shrimp, pineapple and cilantro. Cook just until heated through. Serve immediately over hot rice.

Makes 4 servings

*Cook shrimp in simmering water 2 to 3 minutes or until pink and firm. Drain; set aside until cool enough to handle. Remove shells; cut along curve of body with sharp knife to remove back vein.

Caribbean Pork Chops

PINEAPPLE ORANGE CRISPY CHICKEN

⅓ cup sesame seeds
1¼ teaspoons dried tarragon,
    crumbled
¼ teaspoon ground cloves
2 chicken breasts, split, skinned
    and boned
1 large clove garlic, pressed
1 egg, beaten
    Salt
½ teaspoon coarsely ground
    pepper
1 tablespoon olive oil
1 can (8¼ ounces) Dole pineapple
    slices
1 Dole orange
½ cup orange juice
1 tablespoon sherry wine
1 to 2 teaspoons cornstarch

In pie plate, combine sesame seeds, 1 teaspoon tarragon and ⅛ teaspoon cloves. Rub chicken breasts with garlic, dip in egg, then sprinkle with salt and pepper. Coat chicken breasts with sesame seed mixture.

In large skillet, brown chicken in oil on both sides. Reduce heat to low, cover and cook 2 minutes. Turn chicken and cook 3 to 4 minutes longer or until cooked through. Remove chicken and keep warm. Drain pineapple; reserve syrup. With vegetable peeler, remove peel from orange in thin strips; reserve. Slice orange. In small bowl, combine reserved syrup, remaining ¼ teaspoon tarragon and ⅛ teaspoon cloves, orange juice, sherry and cornstarch. Stir into skillet; add reserved orange peel. Cook, stirring, until sauce boils and thickens. Add pineapple and orange slices; heat through. Serve sauce over fruit and chicken.

Makes 4 servings

CARIBBEAN PORK CHOPS

The exotic ingredients of the Caribbean make these pork chops a favorite.

1 green-tip, large Dole banana
1 tablespoon vegetable oil
2 boneless loin pork chops, 1 inch
    thick
1 large clove garlic, pressed
2 tablespoons slivered fresh
    ginger root
½ cup canned coconut milk
¼ cup water
2 tablespoons chutney
⅛ teaspoon cayenne pepper
1 tablespoon lime juice
    Shredded lettuce or hot cooked
    rice, optional

Cut banana in half crosswise, then lengthwise. In skillet, saute banana in oil 30 to 45 seconds, shaking skillet. Remove banana. Add more oil to skillet if necessary. Brown pork chops on each side 2 to 3 minutes. Stir in garlic and ginger; saute lightly. Stir in coconut milk, water, chutney and cayenne. Spoon over pork chops. Cover; simmer 8 to 10 minutes. Stir in lime juice. Remove from heat. Serve over shredded lettuce or with rice, if desired. Generously spoon sauce over pork chops and bananas.

Makes 2 servings

FIRE AND ICE CHILI

Your family and friends will love this variation of traditional chili.

1 can (20 ounces) Dole pineapple
   chunks
1 can (28 ounces) whole tomatoes
1 can (6 ounces) tomato paste
1 can (4 ounces) diced green
   chiles
2 medium yellow onions, chopped
1 Dole green bell pepper, seeded
   and chopped
3 cloves garlic, pressed or minced
¼ cup chili powder
4 teaspoons ground cumin
1 tablespoon diced jalapeño
   chiles*
2 teaspoons salt
2 tablespoons olive oil
2 pounds lean boneless pork butt,
   cut into 1-inch cubes
  Condiments: small bowls of
   sliced green onions, shredded
   Cheddar cheese and dairy
   sour cream

Drain pineapple; reserve juice. Drain and chop tomatoes; reserve juice. In large bowl, combine reserved juices, tomatoes, tomato paste, green chiles, 1 onion, green pepper, 2 cloves garlic, chili powder, cumin, jalapeño chiles and salt.

In Dutch oven, heat oil until very hot. Brown ¼ of the pork in oil. Remove from pot. Repeat with remaining pork. Return browned pork to pot; add remaining 1 onion and 1 clove garlic. Cook until onion is soft. Add tomato mixture to pork mixture. Cover and simmer 2½ hours, stirring occasionally. Stir in pineapple; cover and simmer 30 minutes longer. Serve with condiments.

Makes 8 to 10 servings

*For more fire, add 2 tablespoons jalapeño chiles.

Fire and Ice Chili

SWEET 'N SOUR

Dole's favorite sweet 'n sour recipe.

1 pound boneless chicken or pork
1 tablespoon vegetable oil
1 medium onion, cut into chunks
2 medium Dole carrots, sliced
1 medium Dole green bell pepper,
    seeded and cut into chunks
2 cans (8 ounces each) Dole
    pineapple chunks, undrained
1 cup catsup
⅓ cup brown sugar, packed
1 clove garlic, pressed
1 tablespoon grated lemon peel
2 tablespoons lemon juice
1 tablespoon soy sauce
1 teaspoon ground ginger
    Hot cooked rice

Cut chicken into ½-inch pieces. In wok or skillet, brown chicken in oil. Reduce heat; stir in onion. Cover; simmer 10 minutes. Stir in remaining ingredients. Cover; simmer 10 minutes longer. Serve with rice.

Makes 4 servings

CARROT SAUTE

1 small clove garlic, pressed
2 tablespoons butter or margarine
1 tablespoon soy sauce
1½ teaspoons water
½ teaspoon sugar
1 cup sliced Dole carrots
½ onion, sliced into chunks
½ cup sliced Dole celery
¼ cup Dole blanched slivered
    almonds, toasted

In large skillet, saute garlic in butter. Stir in soy sauce, water and sugar; bring to a boil. Add carrots, onion and celery; saute until tender-crisp. Sprinkle with nuts.

Makes 2 servings

GREEN & WHITE STIR-FRY

¼ cup sesame seeds, toasted
3 tablespoons soy sauce
3 tablespoons dry sherry
3 tablespoons sesame oil
1 tablespoon sugar
1 teaspoon minced fresh ginger
    root
⅛ teaspoon pepper
2 whole chicken breasts, skinned
    and boned
1 bunch Dole broccoli
1 head Dole cauliflower
3 tablespoons vegetable oil
1½ to 2 teaspoons cornstarch

In large bowl, combine sesame seeds, soy sauce, sherry, sesame oil, sugar, ginger and pepper. Cut chicken into bite-size pieces. Add to soy mixture and marinate in refrigerator at least 1 hour.

Cut broccoli into flowerets. Peel stems and cut crosswise into ⅛-inch-thick slices. Cut cauliflower into flowerets. In wok or large skillet, heat vegetable oil. Stir-fry broccoli and cauliflower 1 minute. Cover; cook 3 minutes. Remove vegetables. Add chicken mixture to wok. Stir and cook until lightly browned, about 3 minutes. Remove chicken. Dissolve cornstarch in small amount of water; add to wok. Cook, stirring, until sauce boils and thickens. Add chicken, broccoli and cauliflower to sauce. Stir and cook 1 minute.

Makes 4 to 6 servings

Sweet 'n Sour

Saucy Fish Fillets

SAUCY FISH FILLETS

*A colorful, tangy fish recipe designed
for your microwave oven.*

**1 can (8 ounces) Dole pineapple
    tidbits
1 tablespoon cider vinegar
1 tablespoon sugar
1½ teaspoons cornstarch
½ teaspoon instant chicken
    bouillon granules
¼ teaspoon ground ginger
    Pinch cayenne pepper
¼ cup sliced green onions
¼ cup sliced water chestnuts
4 white fish fillets, about ½ inch
    thick
2 tablespoons butter or
    margarine, melted
½ cup flavored cracker crumbs
    Paprika**

Drain pineapple; reserve juice. To
make sauce, add enough water to
juice to make ⅔ cup liquid. In
1½-quart microwave-safe bowl, whisk
together juice mixture, vinegar, sugar,
cornstarch, bouillon, ginger and
cayenne. Microwave on HIGH 4 to 5
minutes or until sauce is thickened and
clear, whisking after 2 minutes to
prevent lumps. Stir in onions, water
chestnuts and pineapple. Set aside.

Arrange fish fillets in 12×8×2-inch
microwave-safe dish with thickest
areas to outside edges of dish. Drizzle
with butter; sprinkle with cracker
crumbs and paprika. Cover with
waxed paper. Microwave on HIGH
5 to 9 minutes, rotating dish after
3 minutes. Fish is done when thin
areas flake easily with fork and thick
areas are fork-tender. Let fish stand 2
to 3 minutes; serve with sauce.

Makes 4 servings

SESAME BROCCOLI

**½ bunch Dole broccoli, cut into
    flowerets
1 tablespoon butter or margarine,
    melted
2 teaspoons sesame seeds, toasted
2 teaspoons soy sauce
    Pinch garlic powder
    Pinch ground ginger**

In large saucepan, cook broccoli in
vegetable steamer basket over boiling
water 5 minutes; drain. In small bowl,
combine remaining ingredients. In
serving bowl, toss broccoli with
sesame mixture.

Makes 2 to 3 servings

PINEAPPLE PIZZA

Pineapple provides a wonderful contrast to spicy sausage.

2 cans (8 ounces each) Dole crushed pineapple
½ cup bottled pizza sauce
1 clove garlic, pressed
1 teaspoon dried oregano, crumbled
½ loaf frozen bread dough, thawed
½ pound Italian sausage, crumbled, cooked
1 small Dole green bell pepper, seeded and sliced
¼ cup chopped green onion
2 cups shredded mozzarella cheese
2 tablespoons grated Parmesan cheese

Preheat oven to 500°F. Drain pineapple well, pressing out excess juice with back of spoon. In small bowl, combine pizza sauce, garlic and oregano. Roll and stretch thawed dough to fit greased 12-inch pizza pan. Spread dough with pizza sauce mixture. Top with sausage, green pepper, onion, pineapple and cheeses. Bake in preheated oven 12 to 15 minutes or until pizza is bubbly and crust is browned.

Makes 4 servings

~~~~~~~~~~~~~~~~~~~~~~~~~~~~~~~

To microwave broccoli or asparagus, wrap vegetables in a wet paper towel and cook on HIGH (100% power) 2 minutes or until tender. The vegetables will be bright green and—an extra bonus—there's no pan to wash.

EIGHT FLAVORS POT ROAST

1 can (20 ounces) Dole pineapple chunks
2½ pounds boneless beef chuck
1 tablespoon vegetable oil
1 small yellow onion, chopped
2 cloves garlic, pressed
1½ cups water
½ cup soy sauce
¼ cup dry sherry
2½ tablespoons brown sugar
2 cinnamon sticks
1 tablespoon minced fresh ginger root
1 teaspoon allspice
1 head Chinese cabbage, cut into quarters*
4 teaspoons cornstarch
2 tablespoons water

Drain pineapple; reserve juice. Trim excess fat from beef. Heat large pot until hot. Add oil, swirling to coat sides. Cook onion and garlic in hot oil, stirring, 1 minute. Add beef; brown 2 minutes on each side.

In medium bowl, combine reserved pineapple juice, 1½ cups water, soy sauce, sherry, sugar, cinnamon, ginger and allspice; pour over beef. Bring to boil; reduce heat and simmer, covered, turning meat occasionally, 1¼ hours. Add cabbage; cook 30 minutes longer, adding pineapple last 5 minutes.

Remove meat, cabbage and pineapple from pot. Slice meat and arrange on serving platter with cabbage and pineapple. Strain remaining broth. Pour 1 cup into saucepan. Dissolve cornstarch in 2 tablespoons water; add to broth. Cook, stirring, until sauce boils and thickens. Pour over beef to serve.

Makes 6 servings

*Or use green cabbage (about 2 pounds).

TASTY PORK RAGOUT

½ pound boneless pork loin
1 small onion, chopped
1 large clove garlic, pressed
½ teaspoon dried rosemary,
    crumbled
2 tablespoons butter or margarine
  Salt and pepper
½ cup water
1 head Dole cauliflower, cut into
    flowerets (2 cups)
1 cup sliced Dole carrots
  Hot buttered noodles

Cut pork into 1-inch cubes. In large
skillet, brown pork with onion, garlic
and rosemary in butter. Sprinkle with
salt and pepper to taste. Stir in water.
Cover; simmer 20 minutes. Add
cauliflower and carrots. Cover; simmer
5 minutes longer or until vegetables
are tender-crisp. Serve over noodles.

Makes 2 servings

CONFETTI FRIED RICE

A riot of colors in one quick main dish.

1 can (20 ounces) Dole pineapple
    chunks
3½ teaspoons vegetable oil
1 egg, beaten
1 carrot, shredded
1 clove garlic, pressed
4 cups cooked rice
1 can (8 ounces) water chestnuts,
    chopped
4 ounces cooked ham, julienne-
    cut
½ cup frozen peas, thawed
⅓ cup chopped green onions
¼ cup soy sauce
¼ teaspoon ground ginger

Drain pineapple. Heat ½ teaspoon oil
in wok or large skillet over low heat.
Add egg and swirl around bottom of
wok until egg sets in 6-inch pancake.
Remove and cool. Cut into ⅛-inch

strips. Heat remaining 3 teaspoons oil
in wok over high heat. Stir-fry carrot
and garlic about 1 minute or until
tender. Add rice, stirring until grains
separate. Reduce heat slightly. Stir in
pineapple, water chestnuts, ham, peas,
onions, soy sauce and ginger; increase
heat and heat through. Gently stir in
egg strips.

Makes 6 servings

HOLIDAY BAKED HAM

1 bone-in smoked ham
    (8½ pounds)
1 can (20 ounces) Dole sliced
    pineapple in syrup
1 cup apricot preserves
1 teaspoon dry mustard
½ teaspoon ground allspice
  Whole cloves
  Maraschino cherries

Preheat oven to 325°F. Remove rind
from ham. Place ham on rack in open
roasting pan, fat side up. Insert meat
thermometer with bulb in thickest part
away from fat or bone. Roast ham in
preheated oven about 3 hours.

Drain pineapple; reserve syrup. In
small saucepan, combine syrup,
preserves, mustard and allspice. Bring
to boil; boil, stirring occasionally, 10
minutes. Remove ham from oven, but
keep oven hot. Stud ham with cloves;
brush with glaze. Using wooden picks,
secure pineapple and cherries to ham.
Brush again with glaze. Return ham to
oven. Roast 30 minutes longer or until
thermometer registers 160°F (about
25 minutes per pound total cooking
time). Brush with glaze 15 minutes
before done. Let ham stand 20
minutes before slicing.

Makes 8 to 10 servings

Chicken Colombia

CHICKEN COLOMBIA

Excellent with plain or curried rice.

2 green-tip, medium Dole
   bananas
2 tablespoons vegetable oil
2 whole chicken breasts, split
   Salt and pepper
2 cloves garlic, pressed
2 tablespoons minced fresh ginger
   root
   Orange peel strips*
½ cup orange juice
½ cup water
2 tablespoons chopped chutney
2 teaspoons cornstarch
   Chopped parsley, optional

Cut bananas in half crosswise, then lengthwise. In large skillet, saute bananas in 1 tablespoon oil 30 to 45 seconds, shaking skillet. Remove bananas. Sprinkle chicken with salt and pepper to taste. Add remaining 1 tablespoon oil to skillet. Brown chicken on both sides in hot oil. Add garlic and ginger; saute. Stir in orange peel and juice, ¼ cup water and chutney. Cover; simmer 20 minutes. Dissolve cornstarch in remaining ¼ cup water; stir into pan juices. Cook until sauce boils and thickens. Arrange chicken and bananas on 4 plates. Generously spoon sauce over chicken. Sprinkle with parsley, if desired.

Makes 4 servings

*Use vegetable peeler to cut thin strips from orange.

PINEAPPLE-TOMATO SALSA AND FISH

A light, colorful entree with the flavors of Mexico.

1 Dole fresh pineapple
1 cucumber, peeled, seeded and diced
1 Dole green bell pepper, seeded and diced
1 Dole tomato, chopped
½ red onion, finely chopped
¼ cup lemon juice
1 clove garlic, pressed
2 tablespoons finely chopped cilantro or parsley
2 tablespoons white wine vinegar
1 tablespoon vegetable oil
2 teaspoons sugar
1 teaspoon salt
1 teaspoon dried dill weed
4 white fish steaks (½ inch thick)
1 tablespoon butter or margarine

Twist crown from pineapple. Cut pineapple lengthwise into quarters. Remove fruit from shells with curved knife. Trim off core and cut fruit into bite-size pieces. In medium bowl, combine half of pineapple with next 12 ingredients (reserve remaining pineapple for another use). In skillet, sauté fish in butter 2 to 3 minutes. Spread pineapple salsa over fish. Cover; simmer 10 minutes or until fish is tender and flakes with a fork.

Makes 4 servings

Pineapple-Tomato Salsa and Fish

For an easy and colorful pasta side dish, toss diced fresh tomatoes, olive oil, finely chopped basil leaves and pressed garlic with steaming drained pasta. Top with Parmesan cheese and freshly ground black pepper.

PASTA PRIMAVERA WITH BLUE CHEESE

Quick, colorful and delicious!

1 bunch Dole broccoli, cut into flowerets
2 cups sliced Dole celery
½ Dole red bell pepper, seeded and sliced
8 ounces fettuccine
2 cups sliced fresh mushrooms
1 clove garlic, pressed
2 tablespoons butter or margarine
1¼ cups half-and-half
4 ounces blue cheese
1 package (3 ounces) cream cheese
1 teaspoon salt
Pinch nutmeg
½ cup walnuts, toasted
Grated Parmesan cheese
Freshly ground pepper

To blanch vegetables, cover broccoli, celery and red pepper with boiling water. Let stand 5 minutes. Drain well. Cook fettuccine according to package directions. Drain well. In saucepan, saute mushrooms and garlic in butter. Remove from saucepan and set aside. Add half-and-half, blue cheese, cream cheese, salt and nutmeg to saucepan. Simmer, stirring, until slightly thickened, about 5 minutes. In serving bowl, toss vegetables, fettuccine, nuts and cream sauce together. Add Parmesan cheese and pepper to taste.

Makes 4 servings

CHINESE PINEAPPLE PORK

1 can (20 ounces) Dole pineapple
    chunks
1 cup water
¼ cup soy sauce
4 teaspoons cornstarch
1 pound pork butt or beef top
    round steak
2 tablespoons vegetable oil
1 yellow onion, quartered
2 large cloves garlic, pressed
2 tablespoons minced fresh ginger
    root or 1 teaspoon ground
    ginger
1 bunch Dole broccoli, cut into
    flowerets
4 green onions, cut into 2-inch
    pieces, optional
1 tablespoon sesame seeds,
    toasted
    Hot cooked rice

Chinese Pineapple Pork

Drain pineapple; reserve ¼ cup juice.
In 1-quart measure, combine reserved
juice, water, soy sauce and cornstarch;
set aside. Cut pork into strips. In large
skillet, brown pork in oil. Add onion,
garlic and ginger; saute about 1
minute. Stir in cornstarch mixture; add
broccoli to skillet. Cook until broccoli
is tender-crisp and sauce boils and
thickens. Add pineapple, green onions
and sesame seeds. Heat through.
Serve with rice.

Makes 4 servings

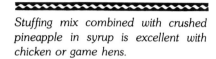

*Stuffing mix combined with crushed
pineapple in syrup is excellent with
chicken or game hens.*

SPICY CHICKEN

2 whole chicken breasts, split
    Salt and pepper
1 egg, lightly beaten
1 cup cornmeal
¼ cup olive or vegetable oil
1 onion, sliced
1 large clove garlic, pressed
1 can (14½ ounces) chicken broth
1 teaspoon chili powder
½ teaspoon ground coriander
¼ teaspoon ground cumin
3 green-tip, large Dole bananas
1 cup halved pimento-stuffed
    olives

Sprinkle chicken with salt and pepper
to taste. Dip in egg and coat with
cornmeal. In skillet, brown chicken in
oil. Remove chicken. Stir in onion and
garlic; saute. Stir in chicken broth, chili
powder, coriander and cumin until
blended. Return chicken to skillet.
Cover; simmer 30 minutes. Slice
bananas; add bananas and olives to
skillet. Spoon juices over and heat
through.

Makes 4 servings

Brazilian Beans and Rice

BRAZILIAN BEANS AND RICE

A wonderful blend of spices and seasonings is accented by sauteed bananas.

3 green-tip, medium Dole bananas
1 large onion, chopped
1 large clove garlic, pressed
2 tablespoons minced fresh ginger root
1 tablespoon vegetable oil
½ pound ground beef
½ pound bulk pork sausage
1 teaspoon ground cumin
¼ teaspoon cayenne pepper
1 can (15¼ ounces) kidney beans
1 can (11 ounces) black bean soup
1 can (8 ounces) stewed tomatoes
2 teaspoons minced cilantro or parsley
4 to 6 cups shredded lettuce
3 to 4 cups hot cooked rice

Cut bananas in half crosswise, then lengthwise. In large skillet, saute onion, garlic and ginger in oil; push to side of skillet. Add bananas; saute 30 to 45 seconds. Remove bananas to plate. Add beef, sausage, cumin and cayenne; brown, stirring in onion mixture. Add undrained beans, soup and tomatoes. Cover; simmer 30 minutes, stirring occasionally. Remove from heat. Stir in cilantro. Place bananas on top. Cover; cook 1 minute. Mound 1 cup lettuce on each plate. Top with ½ cup rice, then bean mixture, spooning bananas to side.

Makes 4 to 6 servings

PINEAPPLE CITRUS GLAZED PORK ROAST

1 boneless pork loin roast (3 to
    4 pounds)
Garlic salt
Pepper
1 can (20 ounces) Dole crushed
    pineapple
1 cup orange juice
½ cup lemon juice
¼ cup sugar
2 tablespoons cornstarch
1 tablespoon grated orange peel
1 tablespoon grated lemon peel
2 teaspoons dried mint, crushed

Preheat oven to 400°F. Place pork on
rack in shallow roasting pan, fat side
up. Sprinkle pork with garlic salt
and pepper to taste. Insert meat
thermometer. Roast in preheated
oven, uncovered, 30 minutes. Reduce
oven to 325°F and roast 30 minutes
longer.

In saucepan, combine undrained
pineapple, orange and lemon juices,
sugar and cornstarch. Cook, stirring,
until mixture boils and thickens. Stir in
orange peel, lemon peel and mint.
Spread half of glaze over pork after 1
hour of roasting. Continue roasting
and baste with glaze every 30 minutes
until thermometer reaches 170°F
(about 2 hours total cooking time).
Remove pork to serving platter. Let
stand 15 minutes before slicing. Serve
with remaining glaze.

Makes 8 servings

Pineapple Citrus Glazed Pork Roast

SWEET 'N SOUR CABBAGE

1 can (11 ounces) Dole Mandarin
    orange segments
6 cups Dole shredded cabbage
1 medium onion, chopped
1 clove garlic, pressed
1 tablespoon vegetable oil
¼ cup white wine vinegar
1 teaspoon caraway seeds
1 teaspoon salt
1 cup Dole fresh pineapple chunks

Drain oranges; reserve ⅓ cup syrup.
In large skillet, saute cabbage, onion
and garlic in oil until onion is soft. Stir
in reserved syrup, vinegar, caraway
seeds and salt. Cover and simmer
10 minutes. Stir in pineapple and
oranges. Cover; cook 5 minutes
longer.

Makes 4 servings

ENTERTAINING WITH STYLE

Backyard Luau

To serve 12

Volcano Punch

Pineapple-Almond Cheese
Spread

Halakahiki Sausage

Luau Fruit Salad

Oven-Roast Pork

Sweet and Tangy Asian Peas

Sweet Potatoes
with Ginger Butter

Tropical Storm Cake

Mango Almond Sponge Cake

VOLCANO PUNCH

3 quarts Dole pineapple juice
2 cans (6 ounces each) frozen
    limeade concentrate
2 quarts ginger ale
2 pints orange or lemon sherbet
Fresh fruit for garnish

In punch bowl, combine pineapple
juice and limeade concentrate. Just
before serving, stir in ginger ale and
add scoops of sherbet. Garnish with
fresh fruit.

Makes about 6 quarts

*Clockwise from top left: Volcano Punch;
Halakahiki Sausage (see page 48);
Pineapple-Almond Cheese Spread
(see page 48)*

HALAKAHIKI SAUSAGE

1 pound smoky link sausage,
  lightly browned
1 can (8¼ ounces) Dole crushed
  pineapple
1 jar (10 ounces) peach preserves,
  apricot jam or orange
  marmalade
1 jar (6 ounces) prepared yellow
  mustard

Cut sausage links diagonally into
bite-size pieces. In small saucepan,
combine undrained pineapple,
preserves and mustard; cook over low
heat 5 minutes. Add sausage and
simmer 15 minutes longer. Turn into
chafing dish, electric frypan or buffet
warmer; serve hot. Provide wooden
picks for serving.

Makes 12 servings

PINEAPPLE-ALMOND
CHEESE SPREAD

2 cans (8 ounces each) Dole
  crushed pineapple
1 package (8 ounces) cream
  cheese, softened
4 cups shredded sharp Cheddar
  cheese
½ cup mayonnaise
1 tablespoon soy sauce
1 cup Dole chopped natural
  almonds, toasted
½ cup finely chopped Dole green
  bell pepper
¼ cup minced green onion or
  chives
  Dole celery stalks or assorted
  breads

Drain pineapple. In large bowl, beat
cream cheese until smooth; beat in
Cheddar cheese, mayonnaise and soy
sauce until smooth. Stir in pineapple,
almonds, green pepper and onion.
Refrigerate, covered. Use to stuff
celery stalks or serve as dip with
assorted breads. Serve at room
temperature.

Makes 4 cups

OVEN-ROAST PORK

4 to 6 pounds boneless pork loin
  roast
4 cloves garlic, pressed or minced
  Salt
  Freshly cracked pepper

Preheat oven to 350°F. Line shallow
roasting pan with heavy aluminum foil
extending 6 inches over edges. Place
pork in center of foil. Rub all sides
with garlic; sprinkle with salt and
pepper to taste. Turn pork fat side up.
Wrap completely with foil and seal so
steam cannot escape.
  Roast in preheated oven 2¾ hours.
Uncover and roast 15 to 20 minutes
longer or until fat is browned. (When
pierced, pork should no longer be
pink.) Slice and spoon a generous
amount of pan juices over each
serving.

Makes 12 servings

*Top to bottom: Oven-Roast Pork; Sweet
Potatoes with Ginger Butter (see page 50);
Sweet and Tangy Asian Peas (see page 50)*

SWEET POTATOES WITH GINGER BUTTER

12 small sweet potatoes
  Vegetable oil
½ cup butter or margarine,
  softened
1 teaspoon ground ginger

Preheat oven to 350°F. Scrub unpeeled sweet potatoes. Rub with vegetable oil; pierce in several places with fork. Place in shallow pan. Bake in preheated oven 30 to 40 minutes or until tender when pierced. In small bowl, beat butter with ginger until fluffy. Spoon into serving bowl. To serve, cut a crosswise gash in top of each potato. Serve ginger butter over sweet potatoes.

Makes 12 servings

SWEET AND TANGY ASIAN PEAS

3 pounds snow peas, ends and
  strings removed
½ cup white vinegar
¼ cup sugar
3 tablespoons sesame seeds,
  toasted
3 to 4 tablespoons soy sauce
2 teaspoons sesame oil

To blanch snow peas, cover with boiling water; let stand 2 minutes. Drain well. To make dressing, combine remaining ingredients. In large bowl, combine snow peas and dressing; toss well. Refrigerate, covered, at least 2 hours.

Makes 12 servings

Luau Fruit Salad

LUAU FRUIT SALAD

1 can (20 ounces) Dole pineapple
  chunks
3 Dole oranges, peeled and
  sectioned
2 apples, cored and chopped
1 papaya, peeled, seeded and cut
  into chunks
1 teaspoon cornstarch
¼ cup vegetable oil
2 tablespoons sugar
2 tablespoons white vinegar
1 tablespoon poppy seeds
1 teaspoon grated orange peel
½ teaspoon paprika
¼ teaspoon salt
5 quarts torn Dole romaine
  lettuce
½ cup Dole blanched slivered
  almonds, toasted

Drain pineapple; reserve juice. In large bowl, combine pineapple, oranges, apples and papaya. For dressing, in saucepan, combine reserved pineapple juice and cornstarch. Cook, stirring, until mixture boils and thickens. Cool. Combine pineapple mixture with oil, sugar, vinegar, poppy seeds, orange peel, paprika and salt in blender. Blend until smooth. Pour dressing over fruit and toss; refrigerate, covered. Just before serving, toss with lettuce and sprinkle with almonds.

Makes 12 servings

MANGO ALMOND SPONGE CAKE

6 eggs, separated
1¼ cups granulated sugar
1 tablespoon lemon juice
½ teaspoon cream of tartar
  Dash salt
1 cup sifted flour
1½ cups chopped peeled mango
½ cup pureed mango (¾ cup chunks)
1 tablespoon orange-flavored liqueur
1 cup whipping cream
2 tablespoons powdered sugar
½ cup Dole blanched slivered almonds, toasted

Preheat oven to 350°F. In large bowl, beat egg yolks, ¾ cup granulated sugar and lemon juice until light and lemon-colored. In large bowl, beat egg whites with cream of tartar and salt until soft peaks form. Stir ¼ of egg whites into egg yolk mixture. Fold remaining egg whites and flour into egg yolk mixture.

Pour batter into greased 9-inch springform pan. Bake in preheated oven 35 to 40 minutes or until cake pulls away from sides of pan. Remove pan to wire rack; cool cake completely. Remove pan sides.

With curved serrated knife, cut 6-inch round from center of cake, leaving shell with 1½-inch-thick sides and ¾-inch-thick base. Tear cake round into small pieces. Process in food processor or blender to make coarse crumbs. On cookie sheet, bake crumbs in 350°F oven 10 minutes or until golden. Let cool.

In bowl, combine chopped mango, pureed mango, remaining ½ cup granulated sugar and liqueur. Spoon into cake shell. Whip cream with powdered sugar until soft peaks form. Spread cream over top of cake. Sprinkle with almonds and toasted crumbs. Reserve any remaining crumbs for other use. Refrigerate 1 hour before serving.

Makes 8 to 10 servings

Mango Almond Sponge Cake

TROPICAL STORM CAKE

2 extra-ripe, large Dole bananas
4 eggs, room temperature
1½ cups sugar
1 cup vegetable oil
¼ cup dark Jamaican rum
1 teaspoon coconut extract
3 cups flour
1½ teaspoons baking soda
1½ teaspoons baking powder
1½ teaspoons ground cinnamon
½ teaspoon salt
1 package (8 ounces) Dole pitted
   dates, chopped
1½ cups coarsely chopped Dole
   almonds, toasted
1 cup flaked coconut
1 cup whole Dole blanched
   almonds, toasted
Rum Glaze (recipe follows)

Preheat oven to 350°F. Puree bananas in blender (1¼ cups). In large mixer bowl, beat eggs. Add sugar and oil; beat 1 minute. Beat in pureed bananas, rum and extract. In medium bowl, combine flour, baking soda, baking powder, cinnamon and salt. Beat into banana mixture until smooth. Stir in dates, 1½ cups chopped nuts and coconut.

Sprinkle 1 cup whole nuts in bottom of greased 10-inch tube pan. Pour in batter. Bake in preheated oven 60 to 65 minutes or until wooden pick inserted in center comes out clean. Cool on wire rack 20 minutes. With spatula, gently loosen cake from side of pan; turn out onto wire rack. Cool completely. Spoon Rum Glaze over top of cake.

Makes 16 servings

Rum Glaze: In saucepan, combine 2 tablespoons butter or margarine, 2 tablespoons rum, 2 tablespoons sugar and 1 tablespoon honey. Heat and stir until melted.

Pre-Game Lunch

To serve 6

Aloha Joes

Potluck Pasta Salad

Hot Buttered Pineapple Smoothie

Hawaiian Splendor Sponge Cake

POTLUCK PASTA SALAD

8 ounces spiral pasta
½ cup vegetable oil
¼ cup white vinegar
1 large clove garlic, pressed or
   minced
2 tablespoons lemon juice
2 teaspoons prepared mustard
2 teaspoons Worcestershire sauce
1 teaspoon salt
Dash pepper
¼ pound snow peas, ends and
   strings removed
2 cups Dole broccoli flowerets
2 cups sliced fresh mushrooms
1 cup Dole cauliflower flowerets
1 cup halved cherry tomatoes

Cook pasta according to package directions. Drain. Meanwhile, in screw-top jar, combine oil, vinegar, garlic, lemon juice, mustard, Worcestershire, salt and pepper. Shake well. In large bowl, combine hot pasta with dressing. Mix well. Add vegetables; toss to coat. Refrigerate, covered.

Makes 8 servings

Top: Potluck Pasta Salad;
bottom: Aloha Joes (see page 54)

ALOHA JOES

1 can (20 ounces) Dole pineapple
   tidbits
1 pound ground beef
1 medium onion, chopped
2 cloves garlic, pressed or minced
½ teaspoon salt
¼ teaspoon pepper
1 can (15 ounces) tomato sauce
2 teaspoons Worcestershire sauce
1 teaspoon chili powder
6 hamburger buns, split and
   toasted

Drain pineapple. In large skillet, brown
meat. Add onion and garlic; cook until
onion is soft. Drain and discard excess
fat. Sprinkle meat mixture with salt
and pepper. Stir in tomato sauce,
Worcestershire and chili powder.
Simmer, uncovered, 15 minutes. Stir
in pineapple. Remove from heat.
Spoon onto buns.

Makes 6 servings

Top: Hot Buttered Pineapple Smoothie;
bottom: Hawaiian Splendor Sponge Cake

HOT BUTTERED
PINEAPPLE SMOOTHIE

5½ cups Dole pineapple juice
¼ cup brown sugar, packed
2 tablespoons butter or margarine
10 whole cloves
3 cinnamon sticks
1 Dole lemon, sliced

In large saucepan, combine pineapple
juice, brown sugar, butter, cloves and
cinnamon sticks. Bring to a boil;
simmer 5 minutes. Add lemon slices.
Serve hot in mugs.

Makes 1½ quarts

HAWAIIAN SPLENDOR
SPONGE CAKE

2 cups flour
1½ cups sugar
1 teaspoon baking soda
¼ teaspoon salt
1 can (20 ounces) Dole crushed
   pineapple
2 eggs, lightly beaten
Golden Frosting (recipe follows)

Preheat oven to 350°F. In large bowl,
combine flour, sugar, baking soda and
salt. Add undrained pineapple and
eggs. Stir until combined. Pour batter
into greased 13×9-inch baking pan.
Bake in preheated oven 30 minutes or
until wooden pick inserted in center
comes out clean. Cool in pan on wire
rack 10 minutes. Spread Golden
Frosting over hot cake in pan.

Makes 12 servings

Golden Frosting: In saucepan,
combine ¾ cup sugar, ¾ cup
evaporated milk, ½ cup butter or
margarine and 1 teaspoon vanilla
extract. Bring to boil; boil about
7 minutes, stirring, until mixture is
thick. Stir in ½ cup chopped nuts and
½ cup flaked coconut.

Parsley Garlic Dip

Picnic Lunch

To serve 6

Parsley Garlic Dip
with Fresh Vegetables

Kamaaina Spareribs

Prepared Macaroni
or Potato Salad

Carrot Pineapple Salad

Black Bottom Cupcakes

PARSLEY GARLIC DIP

1½ cups parsley sprigs
½ cup mayonnaise
1 clove garlic, pressed
3 tablespoons olive oil
3 tablespoons grated Parmesan
  cheese
Assorted fresh vegetables

Combine parsley, mayonnaise, garlic, oil and Parmesan cheese in food processor or blender. Process until well blended. Refrigerate; serve with fresh vegetables.

Makes 1 cup

Kamaaina Spareribs

KAMAAINA SPARERIBS

4 pounds lean pork spareribs
  Salt and pepper
1 can (20 ounces) Dole crushed
  pineapple, drained
1 cup catsup
½ cup brown sugar, packed
⅓ cup red wine vinegar
¼ cup soy sauce
1 teaspoon ground ginger
½ teaspoon dry mustard
¼ teaspoon garlic powder

Have butcher cut across rib bones to make strips 1½ inches wide. Preheat oven to 350°F. Place ribs close together in single layer in baking pan. Sprinkle with salt and pepper to taste. Cover tightly with aluminum foil. Bake in preheated oven 1 hour. Uncover; pour off and discard drippings. In bowl, combine remaining ingredients. Spoon sauce over ribs. Grill over hot coals 15 minutes or bake, uncovered, 30 minutes longer or until ribs are tender and glazed.

Makes 6 servings

CARROT PINEAPPLE SALAD

1 Dole fresh pineapple
1 honeydew melon
3 large Dole carrots, thinly sliced
½ cup thinly sliced Dole pitted dates
Honey-Lime Vinaigrette (recipe follows)

Twist crown from pineapple. Cut pineapple lengthwise into quarters. Remove fruit from shells with curved knife. Trim off core and cut fruit into chunks. Cut melon in half; scoop out seeds and cut fruit into 1-inch pieces. In salad bowl, combine pineapple, melon, carrots and dates. Toss with Honey-Lime Vinaigrette; garnish with lime slices, if desired.

Makes 6 servings

Honey-Lime Vinaigrette: In small bowl, combine ¼ cup honey, 2 tablespoons *each* white wine vinegar and lime juice, 1 tablespoon vegetable oil, and 2 teaspoons grated lime peel. Whisk until blended.

BLACK BOTTOM CUPCAKES

2 packages (3 ounces each) cream cheese, softened
1⅓ cups sugar
1 egg
1 package (6 ounces) chocolate chips
1½ cups flour
¼ cup unsweetened cocoa
1 teaspoon baking soda
½ teaspoon salt
2 extra-ripe, medium Dole bananas
⅓ cup vegetable oil
1 teaspoon vanilla extract
1 firm, large Dole banana

Preheat oven to 350°F. Line 18 muffin cups with paper liners. In small bowl, beat cream cheese and ⅓ cup sugar until light and fluffy. Add egg; beat until well blended. Stir in chocolate chips. Set aside.

In large bowl, combine remaining 1 cup sugar, flour, cocoa, baking soda and salt; mix well. Puree extra-ripe bananas in blender (1 cup). Combine pureed bananas with oil and vanilla. Stir banana mixture into dry ingredients until smooth.

Divide batter evenly among prepared muffin cups. Thinly slice firm banana; place 2 slices in center of batter in each muffin cup. Divide cream cheese mixture evenly over bananas in muffin cups. Bake in preheated oven 30 minutes or until wooden pick inserted in center comes out clean. Cool in pan on wire rack.

Makes 18 cupcakes

Black Bottom Cupcakes

Light Summer Dinner

To serve 4

Steamed Seafood
Garden Platter with
Sesame Ginger Sauce

Crusty French Bread with
Butter

Pineapple Lime Tart

Iced Tea

PINEAPPLE LIME TART

Macaroon Crust (recipe follows)
1 envelope unflavored gelatin
⅓ cup canned cream of coconut
¼ cup lime juice
2 packages (3 ounces each)
    cream cheese, softened
1 carton (8 ounces) plain yogurt
1 cup sugar
2 teaspoons grated lime peel
1 Dole fresh pineapple
¾ cup water
2 teaspoons cornstarch

Clockwise from top left: Pineapple Lime Tart; Sesame Ginger Sauce; Steamed Seafood Garden Platter

Prepare Macaroon Crust. To make filling, in saucepan, sprinkle gelatin over combined cream of coconut and lime juice. Let stand 5 minutes or until gelatin has softened. Heat over low heat, stirring constantly, until gelatin dissolves. Cool. In large bowl, beat cream cheese, yogurt and ¾ cup sugar until fluffy. Beat in cooled gelatin mixture and 1 teaspoon lime peel. Pour filling into prepared crust. Refrigerate until set.

To prepare topping, twist crown from pineapple. Cut pineapple lengthwise into quarters. Remove fruit from shell with curved knife. Trim off core and cut fruit into chunks. In saucepan, combine water, remaining ¼ cup sugar and cornstarch; stir until cornstarch is dissolved. Cook, stirring, until sauce is clear and thickened. Refrigerate. Stir in 3 cups pineapple chunks (reserve any remaining pineapple for another use) and remaining 1 teaspoon lime peel. Spoon topping over pie. Refrigerate until ready to serve.

Makes 6 servings

Macaroon Crust: Preheat oven to 350°F. In bowl, combine 2 cups crisp macaroon cookie crumbs and ¼ cup melted butter or margarine; mix well. Press evenly onto bottom and sides of 9-inch tart pan with removable bottom. Bake in preheated oven 10 minutes. Cool before filling.

When buying pineapple, look for a bright green crown, flat shiny eyes and plump firm fruit. Avoid pineapple with a fermented aroma.

STEAMED SEAFOOD GARDEN PLATTER

The best piece of equipment to use for this recipe is a 5½-quart stockpot with steamer insert. You may also use a steamer basket with the center post removed.

2 cups Dole broccoli flowerets
2 cups Dole cauliflower flowerets
2 cups diagonally sliced Dole celery
2 cups snow peas, ends and strings removed
1 Dole red bell pepper, seeded and sliced
1½ to 2 pounds halibut steaks or other firm, white fish
Salt and pepper
1 green onion, cut into 2-inch lengths
2 tablespoons slivered fresh ginger root
2 tablespoons soy sauce
Sesame Ginger Sauce (recipe follows)

Cook broccoli, cauliflower, celery, snow peas and red pepper in large steamer basket over boiling water 7 to 10 minutes or until tender-crisp. Remove vegetables and keep warm.

Arrange fish in 10-inch glass pie plate. Sprinkle with salt, pepper, onion, ginger and soy sauce. Place pie plate in steamer; cook 12 to 15 minutes or until fish turns opaque. Remove fish to serving platter. Arrange vegetables around fish. Top with 3 tablespoons fish pan juices. Serve with Sesame Ginger Sauce.

Makes 4 servings

Sesame Ginger Sauce: In bowl, combine 3 tablespoons soy sauce, 2 tablespoons white vinegar, 1 teaspoon minced fresh ginger root, ½ teaspoon sesame oil and ½ teaspoon sugar. Stir well to blend.

Outdoor Barbecue

To serve 8

Grilled French Bread

Sweet and Spicy Chicken
Barbecue

Sunflower Seed Cole Slaw

Rainbow Fruit Salad

Banana Split Ice Cream Pie

Summertime Punch

SUNFLOWER SEED COLE SLAW

1 can (20 ounces) Dole pineapple
   tidbits
½ pound Dole carrots, shredded
¼ pound Dole green cabbage,
   shredded
¼ pound red cabbage, shredded
½ cup sunflower seeds, lightly
   toasted
½ cup mayonnaise
2 tablespoons Dole frozen
   pineapple-orange juice
   concentrate
¼ teaspoon salt
   Pinch white pepper

Drain pineapple; reserve 2
tablespoons juice. In bowl, combine
pineapple, carrots, green and red
cabbage and sunflower seeds. To
make dressing, in 1-quart measure,
combine mayonnaise, juice
concentrate, reserved pineapple juice,
salt and pepper. Pour over salad
mixture and toss. Refrigerate, covered,
until ready to serve.

Makes 8 servings

SWEET AND SPICY CHICKEN BARBECUE

1½ cups Dole pineapple orange
   juice
1 cup orange marmalade
⅔ cup teriyaki sauce
½ cup brown sugar, packed
½ teaspoon ground cloves
½ teaspoon ground ginger
4 frying chickens (about 2 pounds
   each), halved or quartered
   Salt and pepper
   Dole pineapple slices
4 teaspoons cornstarch

In saucepan, combine juice,
marmalade, teriyaki sauce, brown
sugar, cloves and ginger. Heat until
sugar dissolves; let cool. Sprinkle
chicken with salt and pepper to taste.
Place in glass baking pan. Pour juice
mixture over chicken; turn to coat all
sides. Marinate, covered, 2 hours in
refrigerator, turning often.

Preheat oven to 350°F. Light
charcoal grill. Drain chicken; reserve
marinade. Bake chicken in preheated
oven 20 minutes. Arrange chicken on
lightly greased grill 4 to 6 inches
above glowing coals. Grill, turning and
basting often with reserved marinade,
20 to 25 minutes or until meat near
bone is no longer pink. Grill pineapple
slices 3 minutes or until heated
through.

In small saucepan, dissolve
cornstarch in remaining marinade.
Cook over medium heat until sauce
boils and thickens. Spoon over
chicken.

Makes 8 servings

*Left: Sunflower Seed Cole Slaw; right:
Sweet and Spicy Chicken Barbecue*

Rainbow Fruit Salad

RAINBOW FRUIT SALAD

2 peaches, peeled, pitted and
  sliced
2 Dole oranges, peeled and sliced
2 cups Dole strawberries, hulled
  and sliced
1 cup Dole seedless grapes
1 cup melon balls
  Pineapple Lime Dressing (recipe
  follows)

In large bowl, combine fruit. Add
Pineapple Lime Dressing; stir gently to
coat.

Makes 8 servings

Pineapple Lime Dressing: In small
bowl, combine ½ cup Dole pineapple
juice, ½ teaspoon grated lime peel,
3 tablespoons *each* lime juice and
honey and 1 tablespoon chopped
crystallized ginger. Whisk until
blended.

SUMMERTIME PUNCH

½ gallon Dole pine-orange banana
  juice
1 pint Dole strawberry sorbet
1 pint Dole strawberries, sliced
1 lime, sliced
  Mint sprigs
1 quart lemon-lime soda
  Ice cubes

Pour juice into punch bowl. With ice
cream scoop, scoop sorbet into punch
bowl. Add strawberries, lime and
mint. Add soda and ice just before
serving.

Makes 3 quarts

BANANA SPLIT ICE CREAM PIE

Chocolate Cookie Crust (recipe
   follows)
1 can (20 ounces) Dole crushed
   pineapple
2 firm, medium Dole bananas
1 quart strawberry ice cream,
   softened
1 cup whipping cream
¼ cup chopped nuts
   Maraschino cherries, optional

Prepare Chocolate Cookie Crust.
Drain pineapple. Slice bananas;
arrange over bottom of crust. Spread
ice cream in even layer over bananas.
Top with pineapple. Whip cream until
soft peaks form. Spread over
pineapple. Sprinkle nuts over whipped
cream. Freeze pie 4 hours or until
firm. Just before serving, garnish with
maraschino cherries, if desired.

Makes 8 servings

Chocolate Cookie Crust: Preheat
oven to 350°F. In bowl, combine
20 finely crushed chocolate sandwich
cookies and ¼ cup melted butter or
margarine. Press evenly onto bottom
and sides of 9-inch pie plate. Bake in
preheated oven 5 minutes. Cool
before filling.

~~~~~~~~~~~~~~~~~~~~~~~~~~~~~~~~~

*Bananas come in various stages of ripe-
ness. Choose the right kind according to
your needs. Green-tipped bananas are
best for sauteing or broiling, while firm
yellow bananas are best for eating out-
of-hand. Ripe, brown-speckled bananas are perfect for baking and blender drinks.*

Banana Split Ice Cream Pie

THIRST
QUENCHERS

CITY SLICKER

*A bubbly, sophisticated thirst
quencher.*

¾ cup Dole pineapple juice
Pineapple juice cubes (see
page 68) or ice cubes
Ginger ale
Dash ground ginger
Cucumber slice, cherry tomato
and lemon slice for garnish

Pour pineapple juice over juice cubes
in glass. Fill with ginger ale. Add
ginger and stir. Garnish with cucumber
slice, cherry tomato and lemon slice.

Makes 1 serving

THE RATTLESNAKE

Bold, composed—then a snap of fire!

3 cups Dole pineapple juice
⅓ cup tomato juice
1 tablespoon powdered sugar
½ to 1 teaspoon liquid hot pepper
sauce
8 pineapple juice cubes (see
page 68) or ice cubes
Lime wedges or slices, optional
Dried red pepper, ripe olive and
lime peel for garnish

In pitcher, combine pineapple juice,
tomato juice, sugar and hot pepper
sauce; blend well. Pour over juice
cubes in glass. Squeeze lime juice into
each drink, if desired. Garnish with
dried red pepper, ripe olive and lime
peel.

Makes 4 servings

Left: City Slicker; right: The Rattlesnake

Mai Tai Slush

FRESH PINEAPPLE DAIQUIRI

1 large Dole fresh pineapple
¾ cup Dole pineapple juice
½ cup light rum
3 ounces frozen limeade
    concentrate
1 cup crushed ice

Twist crown from pineapple. Cut pineapple lengthwise into quarters. Remove fruit from shells with curved knife. Trim off core and cut fruit into chunks. Freeze half the pineapple until firm. (Refrigerate remaining pineapple for another use.) Combine half the frozen pineapple with pineapple juice, rum and limeade concentrate in blender. Blend until smooth. Add remaining frozen pineapple and ice; blend until frothy.

Makes 1 quart

HARVEST FRUIT SIP

5½ cups Dole pineapple juice
½ cup Dole dried dates
½ cup dried prunes
½ cup Dole raisins
3 sticks cinnamon, broken
2 teaspoons vanilla extract

In saucepan, combine all ingredients; heat to a simmer. Remove from heat; allow to steep, covered, overnight in refrigerator to develop flavor. Simmer 15 to 20 minutes. Strain before serving.

Makes 6 servings

One ¾-cup serving of Dole pineapple juice or juice blends provides 100% of the U.S.D.A. daily requirement for vitamin C.

MAI TAI SLUSH

1½ cups Dole pineapple juice
1 pint lemon sherbet
2 ounces rum
2 tablespoons triple sec
1 cup crushed ice
    Lime slices for garnish, optional

Combine pineapple juice, sherbet, rum and triple sec in blender. Add ice; blend until slushy. Garnish with lime slices, if desired.

Makes 2 servings

Pineapple Margarita

QUICK BANANA MALT

A special after-school treat for children.

1 ripe, medium Dole banana, frozen*
¾ cup milk
3 tablespoons chocolate malted milk powder

Slice banana; puree with remaining ingredients in blender.

Makes 1 serving

*Peel banana and freeze overnight in airtight plastic bag.

Quick Banana Malt

PINEAPPLE MARGARITA

⅓ cup Dole pineapple juice
1½ ounces tequila
1 ounce triple sec
Juice of 1 lemon
Crushed ice

Combine pineapple juice, tequila, triple sec and lemon juice in blender. Add ice; blend until slushy. Serve in frosted glass. (Do not put salt on rim.)

Makes 1 serving

PACIFIC SUNSET

3 cups Dole pineapple orange juice
Ice cubes
2 tablespoons grenadine syrup
Fresh fruit for garnish

Pour pineapple orange juice over ice cubes in glasses. Add 1 tablespoon grenadine to each glass. Garnish with fresh fruit.

Makes 2 servings

CHECKMATE

Healthful, delicious—with an exotic flavor.

3 cups Dole pineapple juice
1½ cups carrot pieces
1½ teaspoons minced fresh ginger root
6 pineapple juice cubes or ice cubes
1 tablespoon frozen orange juice concentrate

Puree pineapple juice, carrots and ginger in blender. Strain through a sieve. Pour strained juice back into blender; add juice cubes and juice concentrate. Blend until smooth.

Makes 4 servings

PINEAPPLE PASSION

A vivacious whirl of pure pineapple juice.

2 cups Dole pineapple juice
8 pineapple juice cubes

Combine pineapple juice and juice cubes in blender; blend until slushy. Garnish as desired.

Makes 2 servings

~~~~~~~~~~~~~~~~~~~~~~~~~~~

To make Pineapple Juice Cubes, pour unsweetened, canned pineapple juice into your ice cube trays. Freeze and use just like regular ice cubes. Juice cubes add an intriguing tart-sweet flavor to iced tea, mineral water, lemonade, wine coolers (especially sangria), fruit juices and punch.

PINEAPPLE MINT TULIP

Bright and sparkling . . . fresh as morning dew.

1 cup Dole pineapple juice
2 tablespoons powdered sugar
1 tablespoon grenadine syrup
1 sprig fresh mint
  Ice cubes or pineapple juice cubes

In 1-quart measure, combine pineapple juice, sugar and grenadine; stir well. Rub mint sprig around inside of tall glass. Partially fill glass with ice cubes; pour in juice mixture.

Makes 1 serving

ISLAND FRUIT COOLER

A taste of the tropics for a hot sunny day.

¾ cup Dole pineapple juice
½ cup guava, papaya or mango juice
¼ cup lemon-lime soda
  Ice cubes
  Fresh fruit for garnish

In pitcher, combine pineapple and guava juices and soda. Pour over ice cubes in glass. Garnish with fresh fruit.

Makes 2 servings

Left to right: Checkmate; Pineapple Passion; Pineapple Mint Tulip

For a quick breakfast or snack drink, blend 1 ripe banana with 1 cup milk or orange juice and 1 teaspoon honey.

QUICK WINK BREAKFAST DRINK

Perfect for breakfast on the run.

1 ripe, medium Dole banana, frozen*
¾ cup milk
1 tablespoon wheat germ
2 teaspoons honey
¼ teaspoon ground cinnamon

Slice banana; puree with remaining ingredients in blender.
                    Makes 1 to 2 servings

*Peel banana and freeze overnight in airtight plastic bag.

Quick Wink Breakfast Drink

Hot Spiced Pineapple Tea

HOT SPICED PINEAPPLE TEA

5½ cups Dole pineapple juice
¼ cup honey
2 cinnamon sticks, broken
2 peppermint tea bags

In saucepan, combine pineapple juice, honey and cinnamon sticks. Bring to boil; boil 1 minute. Remove from heat. Add tea bags; steep 2 to 5 minutes. Remove tea bags and cinnamon before serving. Garnish as desired.
                    Makes 6 servings

PINEAPPLE VELVET

Delightful, with a tropical pineapple gusto!

2 cups Dole pineapple juice
½ cup frozen raspberries
¼ cup vanilla yogurt
4 pineapple juice cubes

Combine pineapple juice, raspberries and yogurt in blender. Add juice cubes; blend until smooth.
                    Makes 2 servings

PINEAPPLE SERENADE

Refreshing, with a spirited dash of chili powder.

2½ cups Dole pineapple juice
½ cup peeled, seeded and diced
    cucumber
1 tablespoon powdered sugar
4 to 6 pineapple juice cubes (see
    page 68) OR crushed ice
Dash chili powder

Combine pineapple juice, cucumber
and sugar in blender. Add juice cubes;
blend until smooth. (If using crushed
ice, puree pineapple juice, cucumber
and sugar; then pour over crushed
ice.) Sprinkle beverages with chili
powder.

Makes 2 servings

Hot Mulled Pineapple Juice

*Steep herb tea in canned pineapple
juice instead of water for a nutritious,
flavorful hot drink.*

GINGER PUNCH

1 can (16 ounces) apricot halves
¼ cup frozen limeade concentrate
¼ cup crystallized ginger, chopped
5½ cups Dole pineapple juice,
    chilled
1 quart ginger ale, chilled
1 lime, thinly sliced

Combine undrained apricot halves,
limeade concentrate and ginger
in blender; blend until smooth. In
punch bowl, combine apricot mixture,
pineapple juice and ginger ale. Stir to
blend. Float lime slices on top.

Makes 3 quarts

HOT MULLED
PINEAPPLE JUICE

*Flavored with fruit and spices, this
drink is perfect for a frosty day.*

5½ cups Dole pineapple juice
1 apple, cored and cubed
½ cup Dole raisins
½ cup brown sugar, packed
2 cinnamon sticks, broken
1 tablespoon grated orange peel
½ teaspoon whole cloves
    Quartered orange slices for
    garnish

In saucepan, combine all ingredients;
simmer 15 minutes. Strain before
serving. Garnish with quartered
orange slices.

Makes 6 servings

PIÑA COLADA

½ cup Dole pineapple juice
3 ounces rum
¼ cup canned cream of coconut
2 cups crushed ice

Combine pineapple juice, rum and cream of coconut in blender. Add ice; blend until slushy.

Makes 2 servings

Piña Colada

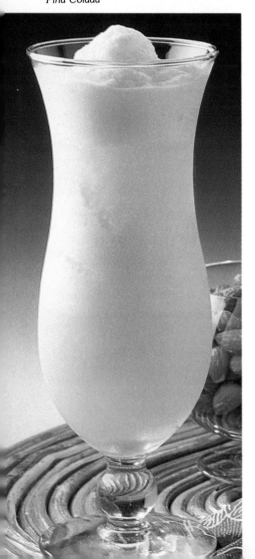

FRUIT PUNCH

A good birthday party punch.

5½ cups Dole pineapple juice, chilled
1 quart apple juice, chilled
1 package (10 ounces) frozen strawberries, thawed
1 quart ginger ale, chilled
  Fresh strawberry slices, lime slices and fresh mint for garnish

In punch bowl, combine pineapple and apple juices. Puree undrained strawberries in blender; stir pureed strawberries into pineapple juice mixture. Pour in ginger ale. Garnish with strawberry slices, lime slices and fresh mint.

Makes 3 quarts

DEVILISH DAIQUIRI

A slow-sipping refresher.

2 ripe, medium Dole bananas*
  Grated peel and juice from 1 lemon
⅓ cup light rum
¼ cup creme de banana liqueur
2 tablespoons powdered sugar
2 cups crushed ice

Slice bananas; combine bananas, lemon peel and juice, rum, liqueur and sugar in blender. Add ice; blend until slushy.

Makes 2 to 4 servings

*Frozen bananas can be used. Peel bananas and freeze overnight in airtight plastic bag.

WAIKIKI COOLER

A nonalcoholic Piña Colada.

1½ cups Dole pineapple juice
⅓ cup canned cream of coconut
1½ teaspoons rum extract
1 cup crushed ice

Combine pineapple juice, cream of coconut and rum extract in blender. Add ice; blend until slushy.

Makes 4 servings

CORAL PUNCH

4½ quarts Dole pineapple orange
    juice
2 quarts lemonade
1 quart cranberry juice
2 cups apple juice
Ice cubes
1 lemon, thinly sliced

In large punch bowl, combine pineapple orange juice, lemonade, cranberry juice and apple juice. Add ice cubes. Float lemon slices on top.

Makes about 2 gallons

PINEAPPLE ORANGE SLUSH

Quick and easy, with the tangy flavor of orange.

3 cups Dole pineapple orange
    juice, chilled
1 pint orange sherbet
1 cup crushed ice

Combine pineapple orange juice and sherbet in blender. Add ice; blend until slushy.

Makes 6 servings

HOW TO MAKE A PINEAPPLE BEVERAGE CUP

1. Twist crown from pineapple.

2. Cut fruit in half crosswise.

3. Trim bottom and top so pineapple halves sit level. Insert sharp knife close to shell and cut around pineapple with a sawing motion.

4. Remove cylinder of fruit; use in beverage or reserve for other use. Makes 2 pineapple beverage cups.

DESSERT DELIGHTS

PIÑA COLADA CHEESECAKE

1½ cups vanilla wafer or graham
   cracker crumbs
½ cup flaked coconut, optional
3 tablespoons butter or
   margarine, melted
1 can (8 ounces) Dole crushed
   pineapple
3 packages (8 ounces each)
   cream cheese, softened
3 eggs
1 cup sugar
1 cup dairy sour cream
3 tablespoons dark rum
2 teaspoons coconut extract
   Pineapple Topping (recipe
   follows)

Preheat oven to 350°. In medium
bowl, combine cookie crumbs,
coconut and butter. Press onto bottom
and sides of 9-inch springform pan.
Bake 10 minutes. Cool.
   Drain pineapple. In large bowl, beat
cream cheese, eggs and sugar. Stir
pineapple, sour cream, rum and
coconut extract into cream cheese
mixture. Pour into prepared crust.
Bake in preheated oven 50 to 55
minutes or until set. Cool to room
temperature; refrigerate until chilled.
Spread Pineapple Topping over
cheesecake just before serving.
Makes 16 servings

Pineapple Topping: In saucepan,
combine 20 ounces (1 can) undrained
crushed pineapple, ½ cup sugar,
1 tablespoon dark rum and
1 tablespoon cornstarch. Cook,
stirring constantly, until thickened and
clear. Cool.

Piña Colada Cheesecake

GINGER MANDARIN SAUCE OVER VANILLA ICE CREAM

Candied ginger and lychee fruit give this dessert an intriguing Oriental flavor.

1 can (20 ounces) lychee fruit
1 can (11 ounces) Dole Mandarin orange segments
1 tablespoon cornstarch
½ cup orange juice
¼ cup sugar
2 tablespoons butter or margarine
2 tablespoons finely chopped crystallized ginger
1 teaspoon grated orange peel
Vanilla ice cream

Drain lychees and orange segments; reserve syrup. In saucepan, dissolve cornstarch in orange juice; add reserved syrup and sugar. Cook, stirring, until sauce boils and thickens. Stir in butter, ginger, orange peel and fruit. Heat through. Serve sauce warm or at room temperature over ice cream. Store leftover sauce in covered container in refrigerator up to 1 week.
Makes 4 cups sauce

SAN FRANCISCO COOKIES

2 ripe, medium Dole bananas
2 cups granola
1½ cups flour
1 cup brown sugar, packed
1 teaspoon ground cinnamon
1 teaspoon baking powder
2 eggs, lightly beaten
½ cup butter or margarine, melted
¼ cup vegetable oil
1 cup chocolate chips

Preheat oven to 350°F. Puree bananas in blender (1 cup). In large bowl, combine granola, flour, sugar, cinnamon and baking powder. Stir in pureed bananas, eggs, butter and oil. Fold in chocolate chips. Spoon batter into ¼-cup measure. Drop onto greased cookie sheet. Spread batter to 2½ to 3 inches. Repeat with remaining batter. Bake in preheated oven 17 minutes or until golden and firm.
Makes 16 to 18 cookies

Ginger Mandarin Sauce over Vanilla Ice Cream

Pineapple Upside-Down Cake

PINEAPPLE UPSIDE-DOWN CAKE

Dole's classic upside-down cake recipe.

1 can (20 ounces) Dole pineapple slices
⅔ cup butter or margarine
⅔ cup brown sugar, packed
10 maraschino cherries
¾ cup granulated sugar
2 eggs, separated
1 teaspoon grated lemon peel
1 teaspoon lemon juice
1 teaspoon vanilla extract
1½ cups flour
1¾ teaspoons baking powder
¼ teaspoon salt
½ cup dairy sour cream

Preheat oven to 350°F. Drain pineapple; reserve 2 tablespoons liquid. In 9- or 10-inch cast iron skillet, melt ⅓ cup butter. Remove from heat.

Add brown sugar and stir until blended. Arrange pineapple slices in skillet. Place 1 cherry in center of each slice.

In large bowl, beat remaining ⅓ cup butter with ½ cup granulated sugar until fluffy. Beat in egg yolks, lemon peel and juice, and vanilla. In medium bowl, combine flour, baking powder and salt. Blend dry ingredients into creamed mixture alternately with sour cream and reserved pineapple liquid. In large bowl, beat egg whites until soft peaks form. Gradually beat in remaining ¼ cup granulated sugar until stiff peaks form. Fold into batter. Spread evenly over pineapple in skillet.

Bake in preheated oven about 35 minutes or until cake springs back when touched. Let stand in skillet on wire rack 10 minutes. Invert onto serving plate. Serve warm or cold.

Makes 8 to 10 servings

BANANA CHOCOLATE CREAM PIE

Banana and chocolate—a fabulous combination—team up in this terrific dessert.

Chocolate Crumb Crust (recipe follows)
2 packages (3½ ounces each) chocolate flavor pudding and pie filling mix (not instant)
1 quart milk
2 ounces unsweetened chocolate, melted
2 firm, large Dole bananas
1 cup whipping cream, whipped

Prepare Chocolate Crumb Crust. In saucepan, combine pudding mix and milk. Prepare pudding mix according to package directions for pie filling. Stir in melted chocolate. Remove from heat. Cool.

Slice bananas. Alternately layer pudding and bananas in prepared crust. Refrigerate until ready to serve. Garnish with whipped cream and additional banana slices, if desired.

Makes 1 pie

Chocolate Crumb Crust: In medium bowl, combine 2 cups chocolate wafer crumbs and ½ cup melted butter or margarine. Press mixture evenly onto bottom and sides of 8- or 9-inch pie plate. Refrigerate until ready to use.

GINGERBREAD UPSIDE-DOWN CAKE

Traditional, but with a spicy style of its own.

1 can (20 ounces) Dole pineapple slices
½ cup butter or margarine, softened
1 cup brown sugar, packed
10 maraschino cherries
1 egg
½ cup dark molasses
1½ cups flour
1 teaspoon baking soda
1 teaspoon ground ginger
½ teaspoon ground cinnamon
½ teaspoon salt

Preheat oven to 350°F. Drain pineapple; reserve ½ cup syrup. In 10-inch cast iron skillet, melt ¼ cup butter. Remove from heat. Add ½ cup brown sugar and stir until blended. Arrange pineapple slices in skillet. Place 1 cherry in center of each slice. In large mixer bowl, beat remaining ¼ cup butter and ½ cup brown sugar until light and fluffy. Beat in egg and molasses. In small bowl, combine flour, baking soda, ginger, cinnamon and salt.

In small saucepan, bring reserved pineapple syrup to boil. Add dry ingredients to creamed mixture alternately with hot syrup. Spread evenly over pineapple in skillet. Bake in preheated oven 30 to 40 minutes or until wooden pick inserted in center comes out clean. Let stand in skillet on wire rack 5 minutes. Invert onto serving plate.

Makes 8 to 10 servings

Banana Chocolate Cream Pie

ALMOND GINGER ICE CREAM PIE

A cool and elegant way to end a perfect meal.

Almond Crust (recipe follows)
1 can (20 ounces) Dole crushed pineapple
1 quart vanilla ice cream, softened
½ cup Dole blanched slivered almonds, toasted
¼ cup crystallized ginger, chopped
3 tablespoons almond-flavored liqueur
1 tablespoon grated orange peel

Prepare Almond Crust. Drain pineapple; reserve all but ½ cup juice. In large bowl, combine pineapple, reserved juice and remaining ingredients. Spoon into prepared crust; freeze overnight or until firm. Let soften slightly before slicing. Garnish as desired.
Makes 8 to 10 servings

Almond Crust: In bowl, combine 1½ cups vanilla wafer crumbs, ⅔ cup toasted ground Dole almonds and ¼ cup melted butter or margarine. Press onto bottom and sides of 9-inch pie plate. Freeze until ready to use.

Almond Ginger Ice Cream Pie

FRESH PINEAPPLE PIE

Fresh pineapple in a nutty cookie crust makes this pie a favorite.

Nut Crust (recipe follows)
1 large Dole fresh pineapple
½ cup sugar
2 tablespoons cornstarch
1 teaspoon grated lemon peel
⅛ teaspoon ground nutmeg
1½ cups water
3 drops yellow food coloring, optional

Prepare Nut Crust. Twist crown from pineapple. Cut pineapple lengthwise into quarters. Remove fruit from shells with curved knife. Trim off core and cut fruit into bite-size chunks. In large saucepan, combine sugar, cornstarch, lemon peel and nutmeg. Stir in water and food coloring. Cook, stirring constantly, until sauce is clear and thickened. Remove from heat. Add pineapple. Cool. Spoon pineapple mixture into prepared crust. Refrigerate, covered, overnight.
Makes 6 to 8 servings

Nut Crust: Preheat oven to 400°F. In large bowl, combine 1¾ cups vanilla wafer crumbs, ⅔ cup ground toasted walnuts, 5 tablespoons melted butter or margarine and 1 tablespoon sugar. Press onto bottom and sides of 9-inch pie plate. Bake in preheated oven 8 minutes. Cool.

The name for pineapple, "ananas," came from an Indian name, "nana," meaning fragrance. Early explorers thought the fruit resembled a pine cone and it came to be known as the "pine of the Indies." "Apple" was added by the English to associate it with juicy, delectable fruits.

Bananas Foster

BANANAS FOSTER

A New Orleans tradition.

4 firm, small Dole bananas
½ cup brown sugar, packed
¼ cup butter or margarine
Dash cinnamon
⅓ cup light rum
Coffee or vanilla ice cream

Cut bananas into halves lengthwise,
then crosswise. In 10-inch skillet, heat
brown sugar and butter until sugar is
melted. Cook and stir 2 minutes or
until slightly thickened. Add bananas;
cook slowly 1 to 2 minutes or until
bananas are heated and glazed.
Sprinkle lightly with cinnamon. Add
rum. Carefully ignite rum with long
match. Spoon liquid over bananas
until flames die out, about 1 minute.
Serve warm over ice cream.

Makes 4 servings

PINEAPPLE ORANGE DESSERT SAUCE

This zesty but subtle sauce is
sensational over ice cream.

1 can (20 ounces) Dole pineapple
chunks, undrained
½ cup orange juice
1 tablespoon cornstarch
1 tablespoon sugar
1 teaspoon ground ginger
1 teaspoon grated orange peel
Vanilla ice cream
Dole blanched slivered almonds,
toasted

In saucepan, combine pineapple
chunks, orange juice, cornstarch,
sugar, ginger and orange peel. Cook
and stir until sauce boils and thickens.
Cool to room temperature. Spoon
sauce over ice cream. Sprinkle with
almonds.

Makes 2 cups sauce

Dessert Delights **81**

Top: Marvelous Macaroons; bottom: Banana Bonanza Ice Cream

MARVELOUS MACAROONS

1 can (8 ounces) Dole crushed
    pineapple
1 can (14 ounces) sweetened
    condensed milk
1 package (7 ounces) flaked
    coconut
½ cup butter or margarine, melted
¾ cup Dole chopped natural
    almonds, toasted
1 teaspoon grated lemon peel
¼ teaspoon almond extract
1 cup flour
1 teaspoon baking powder

Preheat oven to 350°F. Drain
pineapple well, pressing out excess
liquid with back of spoon. In large
bowl, combine pineapple, condensed
milk, coconut, butter, nuts, lemon peel
and extract. In small bowl, combine
flour and baking powder. Beat into
pineapple mixture until blended.

    Drop heaping tablespoons of batter
1 inch apart onto greased cookie
sheets. Bake in preheated oven 13 to
15 minutes or until lightly browned.
Cool on wire rack. Store in covered
container in refrigerator.

              Makes 3½ dozen cookies

BANANA BONANZA ICE CREAM

2 cups milk
2 cups whipping cream
2 eggs, beaten
1¼ cups sugar
2 extra-ripe, medium Dole bananas
½ teaspoon vanilla extract
¼ teaspoon salt
⅛ teaspoon ground nutmeg

In large saucepan, combine milk, cream, eggs and sugar. Cook and stir over low heat until mixture thickens slightly and coats metal spoon. Cool to room temperature. Puree bananas in blender (1 cup). In large bowl, combine cooled custard, pureed bananas, vanilla, salt and nutmeg. Pour into ice cream freezer can. Freeze according to manufacturer's directions.

Makes 2 quarts

BANANA MOCHA LAYERED DESSERT

Ready in minutes—and oh, so good!

1 cup whipping cream
2 tablespoons sugar
1 teaspoon instant coffee powder
½ teaspoon vanilla extract
3 firm, medium Dole bananas
1 package (8½ ounces) chocolate wafer cookies

In large mixer bowl, beat cream, sugar, coffee powder and vanilla until stiff peaks form. Slice bananas. Crumble half the wafers into bottom of 8-inch square pan. Top with half the banana slices. Spread with half the mocha cream. Repeat layers. Refrigerate until ready to serve. Garnish with additional banana slices, if desired.

Makes 8 servings

PINEAPPLE DREAM BARS

½ cup butter or margarine, softened
1 cup dark brown sugar, packed
1⅓ cups flour
1 can (8¼ ounces) Dole crushed pineapple
2 eggs
1 teaspoon baking powder
1 teaspoon ground cinnamon
¼ teaspoon ground nutmeg
¼ teaspoon salt
1 teaspoon rum extract
1½ cups flaked coconut
1 cup chopped walnuts
½ cup chopped maraschino cherries

Preheat oven to 350°F. In medium mixer bowl, beat butter and ⅓ cup brown sugar. Blend in 1 cup flour until mixture is crumbly. Pat into bottom of 13×9-inch baking pan. Bake in preheated oven 10 to 15 minutes or until golden. Keep oven hot, but remove pan to cool.

Drain pineapple well, pressing out excess liquid with back of spoon. In large bowl, beat eggs with remaining ⅔ cup brown sugar until thick. In small bowl, combine remaining ⅓ cup flour, baking powder, cinnamon, nutmeg and salt. Stir dry ingredients and extract into egg mixture. Fold in pineapple, coconut, nuts and cherries. Spread over baked crust. Bake 30 minutes longer or until set. Cool slightly on wire rack before cutting into bars.

Makes 18 bars

Upside-Down Carrot Cake

UPSIDE-DOWN CARROT CAKE

An unusual combination of two classic American cakes.

1 can (20 ounces) Dole pineapple slices
½ cup butter or margarine
½ cup brown sugar, packed
½ cup Dole raisins
¾ cup granulated sugar
2 eggs
1 teaspoon vanilla extract
1 cup shredded Dole carrots
1½ cups flour
½ teaspoon baking powder
½ teaspoon baking soda
½ teaspoon ground cinnamon
½ teaspoon salt
¼ teaspoon ground ginger
½ cup finely chopped walnuts

Preheat oven to 350°F. Drain pineapple; reserve ½ cup liquid. In 10-inch cast iron skillet, melt ¼ cup butter. Remove from heat. Add brown sugar and stir until blended. Arrange pineapple slices in skillet and sprinkle with raisins.

In large mixer bowl, beat remaining ¼ cup butter with granulated sugar until light and fluffy. Beat in eggs and vanilla; beat in carrots. In medium bowl, combine flour, baking powder, baking soda, cinnamon, salt and ginger. Stir in nuts. Beat into creamed mixture alternately with reserved liquid, ending with dry ingredients. Spread evenly over pineapple in skillet. Bake in preheated oven 40 to 45 minutes or until wooden pick inserted in center comes out clean. Let stand in skillet on wire rack 5 minutes. Invert onto serving plate.

Makes 8 to 10 servings

FRESH PINEAPPLE MELBA

A colorful blend of wonderfully rich flavors.

2 packages (10 ounces each) frozen raspberries, thawed
Sugar
2 tablespoons cornstarch
3 tablespoons raspberry-flavored brandy
1 Dole fresh pineapple
3 cups (1½ pints) vanilla ice cream
Fresh raspberries for garnish, optional

In 2-quart saucepan, combine raspberries and their juice, sugar to taste and cornstarch. Stir until cornstarch is dissolved. Cook over medium heat, stirring constantly, until sauce turns clear and is slightly thickened. Remove from heat. Stir in brandy. Place plastic wrap directly on surface of sauce to cover. Refrigerate.

Twist crown from pineapple. Cut pineapple lengthwise into quarters. Remove fruit from shells with curved knife. Trim off core and cut fruit into chunks. Refrigerate, covered, until serving time.

To serve, spoon pineapple into 6 dessert dishes. Top each with scoop of ice cream. Drizzle with raspberry sauce; garnish with fresh raspberries, if desired.

Makes 6 servings

Fresh Pineapple Melba

PINEAPPLE PECAN BARS

2⅓ cups flour
⅔ cup powdered sugar
1 cup butter or margarine, diced
1 can (20 ounces) Dole crushed
     pineapple
4 eggs, lightly beaten
¾ cup brown sugar, packed
2 cups coarsely chopped pecans

Preheat oven to 350°F. In large bowl, combine 2 cups flour and powdered sugar. Cut in butter until mixture is crumbly. Using bottom of metal measuring cup, pat dough into 13×9-inch baking pan. Bake in preheated oven 15 minutes. Keep oven hot, but remove pan to cool slightly.

Drain pineapple. In medium bowl, combine remaining ⅓ cup flour, pineapple, eggs and brown sugar. Stir in pecans. Pour over partially baked crust. Bake 30 to 35 minutes longer. Cool completely on wire rack before cutting into bars.

Makes 16 to 24 bar cookies

Pineapple Pecan Bars

HAWAIIAN TRIFLE

2 packages (3⅛ ounces each)
     vanilla flavor pudding and pie
     filling mix (not instant)
2 cups milk
1½ cups Dole pineapple juice
2 cups whipping cream
1 package (16 ounces) frozen
     pound cake, thawed
½ cup cream sherry
1 cup raspberry jam, melted
1 can (20 ounces) Dole crushed
     pineapple
Maraschino cherries, optional

Prepare pudding mix according to package directions, using milk and pineapple juice as liquid. Place saucepan in bowl of ice water to cool pudding; stir often. In medium bowl, beat 1 cup cream until soft peaks form; fold into cooled pudding. Cut pound cake in half lengthwise. Drizzle sherry over cake; cut cake into chunks.

Spoon 1 cup pudding into 2½- to 3-quart glass serving bowl. Top with half the cake and half the jam. Reserve ½ cup undrained pineapple for garnish. Spoon half the remaining pineapple on top of jam in serving bowl. Spoon half the remaining pudding on top. Repeat layering with remaining ingredients, ending with pudding. Refrigerate, covered, overnight.

In medium bowl, beat remaining 1 cup cream until soft peaks form; spread over top of trifle. Drain reserved ½ cup pineapple. Garnish trifle with pineapple and maraschino cherries, if desired.

Makes 8 servings

If you have ripe, brown-speckled bananas and don't have an immediate use for them, simply peel them, wrap the fruit with plastic and store in the freezer. Frozen bananas taste great in milk or juice shakes, and they thaw easily for baking. You can also freeze pureed bananas in a plastic container.

Pineapple Raisin Jumbles

BANANA BREAD PUDDING

2 extra-ripe, medium Dole
    bananas
4 slices bread, cubed
¼ cup Dole raisins
1¼ cups milk
2 firm, medium Dole bananas
2 eggs, lightly beaten
½ cup sugar
1 tablespoon butter or margarine,
    softened
1 teaspoon vanilla extract
½ teaspoon ground nutmeg
¼ teaspoon salt

Preheat oven to 350°F. Puree extra-ripe bananas in blender (1 cup). In large bowl, combine bread cubes and raisins. Stir in pureed bananas and milk. Let stand 5 minutes. Slice firm bananas; stir into bread mixture. Stir in eggs, sugar, butter, vanilla, ¼ teaspoon nutmeg and salt. Pour into greased 1½-quart casserole dish. Sprinkle with remaining ¼ teaspoon nutmeg. Place casserole in large pan. Pour boiling water into pan to come 2 inches up sides of casserole. Bake in preheated oven 1 hour. Serve warm.
Makes 8 servings

PINEAPPLE RAISIN JUMBLES

Surprise your kids with this delightful lunch-box treat.

2 cans (8 ounces each) Dole
    crushed pineapple
½ cup butter or margarine,
    softened
½ cup sugar
1 teaspoon vanilla extract
1 cup flour
4 teaspoons grated orange peel
1 cup Dole blanched slivered
    almonds, toasted
1 cup Dole raisins

Preheat oven to 350°F. Drain pineapple. In large bowl, beat butter and sugar until light and fluffy. Stir in pineapple and vanilla. Beat in flour and orange peel. Stir in almonds and raisins. Drop heaping tablespoons of batter 2 inches apart onto greased cookie sheets. Bake in preheated oven 20 to 22 minutes or until firm. Cool on wire rack.
Makes 2 to 2½ dozen cookies

Tropical Crisp

TROPICAL CRISP

1 Dole fresh pineapple
4 Dole bananas
1 cup brown sugar, packed
1 cup flour
¾ cup rolled oats
½ cup flaked coconut
½ teaspoon ground nutmeg
½ cup butter or margarine,
  softened

Preheat oven to 350°F. Twist crown from pineapple. Cut pineapple lengthwise into quarters. Remove fruit from shells with curved knife. Trim off core and cut fruit into chunks. Cut bananas into chunks. In 9-inch baking dish, toss bananas and pineapple with ¼ cup brown sugar. In medium bowl, combine remaining ¾ cup brown sugar, flour, oats, coconut and nutmeg. Cut in butter until crumbly. Sprinkle over fruit mixture. Bake in preheated oven 45 to 50 minutes or until topping is crisp and juices have begun to bubble around edges.

Makes 8 servings

PINEAPPLE MACADAMIA CHEESEPIE

A prize winner from a recent Dole recipe contest.

Macadamia Crust (recipe
   follows)
1 can (8 ounces) Dole crushed
   pineapple
12 ounces cream cheese, softened
¾ cup plain yogurt
½ cup sugar
1 egg
1 teaspoon vanilla extract

Prepare Macadamia Crust. Preheat oven to 350°F. Drain pineapple well, pressing out excess liquid with back of spoon. In medium mixer bowl, beat cream cheese until smooth; beat in yogurt, sugar, egg and vanilla. Spread pineapple over prepared crust, reserving 2 tablespoons for garnish. Pour filling over pineapple. Bake in preheated oven 20 minutes. Cool on wire rack; refrigerate at least 2 hours. Just before serving, garnish with reserved pineapple.

Makes 6 servings

Macadamia Crust: In medium bowl, combine 1 cup chopped macadamia nuts, ¾ cup graham cracker crumbs, 6 tablespoons melted butter or margarine and 2 tablespoons sugar. Press onto bottom and sides of 8-inch pie plate. Refrigerate until ready to use.

〰〰〰〰〰〰〰〰〰〰〰〰〰

Toasting heightens the flavor of almonds. Spread them flat in a baking pan or jelly roll pan and toast them in a 350°F oven about 10 minutes or until lightly browned.

Jungle Bars

JUNGLE BARS

Kids will love this healthful no-bake snack.

2 ripe, medium Dole bananas
8 ounces dried figs
8 ounces dried apricots
8 ounces Dole pitted dates
8 ounces Dole raisins
2 cups granola
8 ounces Dole chopped natural
   almonds, toasted
1 cup flaked coconut

Coarsely chop bananas, figs, apricots, dates, raisins and granola in food processor or run through food grinder. Stir in almonds. Press mixture into greased 13×9-inch baking dish. Sprinkle with coconut. Cover; refrigerate 24 hours to allow flavors to blend. Cut into squares.

Makes 24 bars

PINEAPPLE CARROT COOKIES

2 cans (8 ounces each) Dole crushed pineapple
¾ cup butter or margarine, softened
½ cup brown sugar, packed
½ cup granulated sugar
1 egg
1 teaspoon vanilla extract
1 cup shredded Dole carrots
1 cup chopped walnuts
1 cup Dole raisins
1½ cups flour
1 teaspoon ground cinnamon
½ teaspoon ground ginger
½ teaspoon baking powder
¼ teaspoon salt

Preheat oven to 375°F. Drain pineapple well. In large mixer bowl, beat butter and sugars until light and fluffy. Beat in egg and vanilla. Beat in pineapple, carrots, nuts and raisins. In medium bowl, combine remaining ingredients; beat into pineapple mixture until well blended. Drop heaping tablespoons of batter 2 inches apart onto greased cookie sheets. Flatten tops with spoon. Bake in preheated oven 15 to 20 minutes or until golden.

Makes 3 dozen cookies

Pineapple Carrot Cookies

BANANA MOCHA CAKE

2 extra-ripe, medium Dole bananas
1 teaspoon instant coffee powder
1¼ cups flour
⅔ cup sugar
¼ cup cornstarch
3 tablespoons cocoa
1 teaspoon baking soda
½ teaspoon salt
⅓ cup vegetable oil
1 egg, lightly beaten
1 tablespoon vinegar
1 teaspoon vanilla extract
Silky Mocha Frosting (recipe follows)

Preheat oven to 350°F. Puree bananas in blender (1 cup). Stir coffee powder into pureed bananas. In 9-inch square baking pan, combine flour, sugar, cornstarch, cocoa, baking soda and salt. Blend well. Make well in center of dry ingredients. Add banana mixture, oil, egg, vinegar and vanilla. Stir in dry mixture with fork until well blended. Bake in preheated oven 30 minutes. Cool completely on wire rack. Spread with Silky Mocha Frosting.

Makes 12 servings

Silky Mocha Frosting: In large mixer bowl, combine 3 tablespoons butter or margarine, 1½ cups sifted powdered sugar, 2 tablespoons cocoa and 1 teaspoon instant coffee powder. Add 2 tablespoons milk and ½ teaspoon vanilla extract. Beat until smooth.

It takes 2 ripe, medium bananas to make 1 cup of pureed banana. One medium banana yields about 1 cup sliced fruit.

Classic Banana Cream Pie

CLASSIC BANANA CREAM PIE

2 eggs
½ cup plus 2 tablespoons sugar
¼ cup flour
2 cups milk, scalded
½ cup unsalted butter or
    margarine
1 tablespoon vanilla extract
5 firm, medium Dole bananas
1 baked 9-inch pastry shell
1 cup whipping cream

In heavy saucepan, beat eggs, ½ cup sugar and flour until pale lemon color. Gradually beat hot milk into egg mixture. Cook, stirring constantly, over medium heat until sauce thickens, about 5 minutes. Remove from heat. Stir in butter and vanilla until blended. Place plastic wrap directly on surface of filling to cover. Cool.

To assemble pie, slice bananas; reserve a few slices for garnish, if desired. Fold remaining bananas into filling; spoon into baked pastry shell. Beat cream with remaining 2 tablespoons sugar until soft peaks form. Spread on top of pie.

Makes 8 servings

EASY STRAWBERRY MOUSSE

2 extra-ripe, medium Dole
    bananas
1 can (20 ounces) Dole pineapple
    slices
1 package (3 ounces) strawberry
    flavor gelatin
1 carton (8 ounces) strawberry
    yogurt
2 cups whipping cream
    Dole strawberry slices for
    garnish

Puree bananas in blender (1 cup).
Drain pineapple; reserve juice. In small
saucepan, bring reserved juice to boil;
remove from heat. Dissolve gelatin in
juice. In large bowl, combine yogurt
and pureed bananas. Blend gelatin
mixture into banana mixture.
Refrigerate until slightly thickened.
    In large mixer bowl, beat cream
until soft peaks form. Fold into gelatin
mixture. Arrange 7 pineapple slices
around sides of clear glass bowl. Turn
gelatin mixture into pineapple-lined
bowl. Refrigerate until firm. Garnish
with remaining 3 pineapple slices and
strawberries.

Makes 8 servings

CHOCOLATE BANANA CAKE

3 extra-ripe, medium Dole
    bananas
1⅓ cups sugar
3 eggs
3 squares (1 ounce each)
    unsweetened chocolate
½ cup butter or margarine
1 tablespoon rum extract
1¾ cups flour
1 teaspoon baking soda
½ teaspoon salt
    Rum Fudge Frosting (recipe
    follows)

Preheat oven to 350°F. Puree bananas
in blender (1½ cups). In saucepan,
combine ½ cup pureed bananas,
⅓ cup sugar, 1 egg and chocolate.
Heat, stirring, until chocolate melts.
Cool. In large mixer bowl, beat
remaining 1 cup sugar and butter until
light and fluffy. Add extract and
remaining 2 eggs, 1 at a time, beating
well after each addition. In small bowl,
combine flour, baking soda and salt.
Beat dry ingredients into butter
mixture alternately with remaining
pureed bananas. Blend in chocolate
mixture.
    Bake in 2 greased and floured
9-inch round cake pans in preheated
oven 25 to 30 minutes or until
wooden pick inserted in center comes
out clean. Cool 10 minutes in pan.
Invert onto wire rack to cool
completely.
    Prepare Rum Fudge Frosting. Cut a
paper-thin slice from top of each cake
so frosting will soak into cake. Frost
1 layer; top with remaining layer,
placing cut side up. Frost sides and
top. Garnish cake with additional
banana slices, if desired.

Makes 8 to 10 servings

Rum Fudge Frosting: Over hot, not
boiling, water, melt 4 ounces semi-
sweet chocolate with 1 tablespoon
butter. Stir in 3 tablespoons light corn
syrup and 1 tablespoon dark or light
rum. Cool to room temperature.
Whisk in ½ cup whipping cream.
Refrigerate until frosting is of
spreading consistency.

HOW TO CUT A PINEAPPLE

EASY CUT

1. Twist crown from pineapple.

2. Cut in half, then in quarters.

3. Trim off ends and core. Remove fruit from shell with a curved knife.

4. Cut into bite-size chunks.

PINEAPPLE BOAT

1. Cut pineapple in half lengthwise through crown.

2. Remove fruit from shell with a curved knife, leaving shell intact.

3. Cut into quarters; remove core.

4. Cut into bite-size chunks.

INDEX